Out of the Blue

Out of the Blue

✦

The story of the Anaheim Angels'
improbable run to the 2002 World Series
title

Joe Haakenson

iUniverse, Inc.
New York Lincoln Shanghai

Out of the Blue
The story of the Anaheim Angels' improbable run to the 2002 World Series title

iUniverse books may be ordered through booksellers or by contacting:

iUniverse
2021 Pine Lake Road, Suite 100
Lincoln, NE 68512
www.iuniverse.com
1-800-Authors (1-800-288-4677)

ISBN-13: 978-0-595-37293-5 (pbk)
ISBN-13: 978-0-595-81691-0 (ebk)
ISBN-10: 0-595-37293-7 (pbk)
ISBN-10: 0-595-81691-6 (ebk)

Printed in the United States of America

Contents

Gene Autry's legacy was evident at Edison Field during the playoffs.
Gene's widow Jackie Autry (center) made sure of it.

1

One for the Cowboy

Tim Salmon had been thinking about it. The 10-year veteran right fielder of the Anaheim Angels was supposed to be hypnotized by his manager's one-day-at-a-time mantra, but he couldn't help himself. "What if we really win it all?" Salmon remembered thinking. "We've got to find a way to get Gene Autry on the field any way we can. What would be reflective of that idea? It was his hat."

If Autry—the Angels' original owner who died in 1998—could not be there in person, his white Stetson could. Salmon made sure of it, requesting a hat from Autry's widow Jackie days earlier and hiding it in a safe place in the Angels clubhouse. After the Angels won Game 7 of the World Series against the San Francisco Giants, Salmon retrieved it, took it onto the field where he held the hat aloft, literally dancing his way around the Edison Field outfield.

The hat eventually made its way to the podium, where Angels shortstop David Eckstein modeled it proudly during the World Series Trophy presentation. Angels manager Mike Scioscia held the trophy aloft and smiled like a proud father. That was a lot for a man like Scioscia, who kept his emotions in check and never let his players see what he felt. It was Oct. 27, 2002. In their 42nd season, with the ghosts of past failures seemingly always haunting them, the Angels won the World Series. Autry didn't live to see his Angels win or even reach the World Series. But so many of these Angels showed Autry's spirit was still with the team.

Autry was both a shrewd businessman and a devoted fan of the game, but he never fulfilled his World Series dream. Until now.

WHAT RIVALRY?

Few from either the Dodgers or Angels will ever admit there has been much of a rivalry between the two clubs, but there is, and always has been. The two teams' original owners became rivals before the Angels even existed.

When Dodgers owner Walter O'Malley pulled back the radio rights in 1960 to broadcast their games on Autry's KMPC, Autry wasn't happy. So when the American League awarded an expansion team to Los Angeles, Autry worked out a broadcasting agreement with the proposed new Angels ownership group that included Bill Veeck.

O'Malley, though, fought to keep the Angels out, worried the Angels would steal some of his business. But after Veeck's group pulled out, Autry got approval from the league and the required permission from O'Malley to purchase the American League's newest entry. Gene Autry owned the Angels.

Though the Angels had good teams, great players and colorful characters over the years, they never reached the World Series. They won American League West Division titles in 1979, '82 and '86, and even came within one strike of the World Series in '86 before they were struck again by failure, blowing a three-games-to-one series lead.

That failure had been so enduring for the franchise that there have been some who truly believed there were more powerful forces at work. There have been rumors that Edison Field, formerly Anaheim Stadium and before that, the "Big A," was built on an Indian burial ground. The Angels were cursed, it was said, and who could argue.

But in 2002, that all changed. Just two days after the Angels' World Series victory in Game 7, one-time Angel Bobby Grich soaked in the energy from a rally that drew 100,000 people. "All the ghosts are gone," he said. "All the jinxes are gone, all the bad vibes are gone. There's nothing but blue skies ahead."

THE DODGER SHADOW

The color blue was never a favorite of the Angels. It's the color of the Dodgers. The Dodgers were here first. The Dodgers won as soon as they got to L.A. They were already successful. Autry's favorite color, Jackie says, was red. But the Angels went with a mix of blue and red, tried different fonts and color schemes before we were introduced to periwinkle blue by the Walt Disney Co., which purchased the Angels from Autry's estate after his death.

But the team, with its pinstripes and fancy new duds, were just that. Duds. They played well in 1995, '97 and '98, but didn't reach the playoffs. Again, it was always something. Gary DiSarcina's thumb. Mo Vaughn's ankle. Something.

So Disney's marketing team came up with a drastic change before the 2002 season. Red. Just red. Autry's red. For the first time in their history, the Angels had no blue in their uniform.

Predictably, the Angels' new look wasn't met with much more than passing curiosity. Just another change for the Angels. Not real consistent over there, those Angels. They've always got something new. New manager, new general manager, new players, new uniforms. They seemed to forever be the Dodgers' little brother.

Playing in the shadow of the Dodgers and escaping an inferiority complex would not be such as easy task. For the Angels, it took 42 years to get over theirs with the Dodgers.

Lacking the tradition and the championship hardware, it had been difficult for the Angels to feel on par with their big brothers a few miles north up Interstate 5. The Angels had their share of big names going back to the 1960s, but when it came time to play the annual Freeway Series after spring training each year, the Angels usually felt like they had to earn the respect of the Dodgers.

"I got the sense that they looked down on us," said Angels right fielder Tim Salmon, who won the American League Rookie of the Year award in 1993, but was overshadowed by the National League Rookie of the Year that season, Dodgers catcher Mike Piazza. "They had good teams, and their big names made us feel like a JV team.

"Before, there was the Piazza craze, and the (Raul) Mondesi craze. But those guys aren't there anymore. They've got some good players there now, but I don't sense that feeling anymore."

Angels vice president and director of communications Tim Mead, who began working for the club in 1980, has had close relationships with many in the Dodgers organization over the years. But soon after he began his career in Anaheim, he noticed a difference in how the two teams were treated by the media.

The Dodgers won the World Series in 1981, and the club was lauded by the local chapter of the Baseball Writers Association of America after the season during its "annual" dinner. The very next year, the Angels reached the American League Championship Series, coming within one win of going to the World Series before losing out to the Milwaukee Brewers. But after that season, Mead said, the writers didn't even have a dinner.

"I don't think the organizations ever competed," Mead said. "A lot of it, and rightfully so, is media generated. It's an L.A.-based media."

Mead, however, admits he is noticing a change in the general perception of the two organizations, one that has them closer to being equal, both on and off the field.

"Part of what you're seeing has to do with Mike Scioscia," Mead said of the Angels manager who played 13 seasons with the Dodgers. "He really has implemented a tremendous program. Mike has brought a lot of (public) support with him. And I think the change of ownership, with both teams, has affected both sides."

Though both teams were owned by corporate giants at the time—the Dodgers under Rupert Murdoch's News Corp. and the Angels under the Walt Disney Co.—the team payrolls were not equal. The Dodgers' payroll at the beginning of 2002 was the fifth highest in baseball at just less than $95 million. The Angels ranked No. 15 at $61 million.

On the field, it couldn't get much closer. With the inception of interleague play in 1997, the Freeway Series began to count for something, and the Angels more than held their own, winning 17 of 33 games through the 2002 season.

But the idea of any real rivalry is still lost in the expanse of a 162-game season. After all, the Dodgers hate the Giants, not the Angels.

"Rivalries are going to exist more so within your division," Scioscia said. "Those are the teams you're trying to get past to win a pennant."

Some of the other intra-city rivalries are more intense, Scioscia said, because there is more of a history between the teams.

"It's not like the Yankees and the Mets or the Giants and the A's, because those teams have played each other in the World Series," Scioscia said. "We haven't had those games with the Dodgers yet."

Under the guidance of Scioscia, about to begin his third season as the Angels manager, something truly different was about to happen. Scioscia and his Angels were about to emerge from the Dodger shadow.

Mike Scioscia became the 17th person in baseball history to win the World Series as both a player and a manager.

2

The Rock

Michael Lorri Scioscia is the youngest of Fred and Florence Scioscia's three children. Fred ran a beer distributorship and Florence was a teacher while raising Mike, older brother Fred and older sister Gail in Morton, Pa. Young Mike could appreciate his parents' work ethic and it has stuck with him. But before he would put into use in his professional career, Mike was just one of the kids in the neighborhood, looking to have some fun. And in his neighborhood, playing sports was it.

"I remember playing sports my whole life," Scioscia said. "One of my first memories is running around playing with friends and playing ball when I was 3 or 4 years old. We played ice hockey, baseball, football and basketball. Everything was seasonal back east."

Athletic success ran in Scioscia's family. Older brother Fred went on to play semi-pro football. Scioscia played football, basketball and baseball at Springfield High. He was named Delaware County player of the year in baseball in both 1975 and 1976, but his goal at the time had to do with football. As a guard on the offensive line in high school, Scioscia hoped to play football at Penn State for legendary coach Joe Paterno.

"A recruiter said I was too small and too slow for guys at that level," Scioscia said.

However, Scioscia did receive an offer to play both football and baseball and the University of Delaware. He also got a full-ride scholarship offer to play baseball at Clemson University, and that seemed to be Scioscia's destination. There was also the option of playing professional baseball. Scioscia was drafted in the first round, the 19th pick overall, in the June, 1976 Major League draft by the Los Angeles Dodgers.

"My mom taught school for 30 years, so she supported going to Clemson," Scioscia said. "My dad said it might be my only opportunity to play pro ball. They were split and so it was up to me."

A month after the baseball draft, Scioscia had not made up his mind, but he was leaning towards going to Clemson. It was July of 1976, and the 17-year-old Scioscia was at home when the phone rang.

"I was two weeks away from going (to Clemson)," Scioscia remembered. "The Dodgers were in town to play the Phillies and I got a call from Tom Lasorda. He was the third-base coach at the time and he invited me to work out at the stadium before one of the games. He said someone would be at my home in an hour to pick me up. I grabbed my spikes and glove and left a note for my parents telling them where I was. I could just imagine my mom reading that note."

The next day, Scioscia was on an airplane to Bellingham, Wash. to begin his professional career with the Dodgers' Rookie League team.

"My mom made sure it was in my contract that the Dodgers would pay for college," Scioscia said.

Scioscia did go to college in the off season following the 1976, '77 and '78 seasons, but he played winter ball in the Dominican Republic in 1979 and '80, which put his academic career on hold. Meanwhile, his baseball career was about to blossom.

PLAY BALL

Scioscia ascended through the Dodgers' minor league system rapidly. He was still only 17 when he played Rookie ball in Bellingham, Wash. in the summer of '76, hitting .278 in 46 games. In 1977, he attended his first major league spring training, reporting to Vero Beach, Fla. at the ripe old age of 18.

"That first spring training was incredible," Scioscia said. "You start to put faces to names. Before then these guys were all mythological to me. Roy Campanella, Sandy Koufax, John Roseboro. I was trading their baseball cards eight months ago, and now I'm in the middle of it."

That first spring would have a lasting effect on Scioscia.

"I took a little part of a lot of people," Scioscia said. "Roy Campanella, Del Crandall and John Roseboro were big influences on me at an early age. Not just giving me a foundation for being a catcher, but what it takes to win."

And there was Lasorda, then the Dodgers manager and head cheerleader.

"Tommy magnified it with communication," Scioscia said. "He'd get a guy to compete at a level higher than that guy thought he could. And he made guys love to work hard. Tommy had a tremendous passion for the game and was a great instructor. He gave you the confidence you could be better. He was a tireless worker with endless enthusiasm."

Scioscia played Class-A ball in Clinton, Iowa, in 1977, then played Class-AA ball in San Antonio, Texas in 1978. His breakout year came in 1979, when Scioscia played at Class-AAA Albuquerque. He played in 143 games, hit .336 with 34 doubles and 68 RBIs. He hit only three home runs, but homers were never Scioscia's forte. Except when it meant a trip to the World Series.

Scioscia spent some of the 1980 season in Albuquerque, but he also made his major league debut that season. On April 20, 1980, Scioscia was the starting catcher for pitcher Don Sutton. Scioscia doubled in his first major league at-bat, off Houston Astros pitcher Joe Niekro. Scioscia also remembers scoring the first run of the game that day on a wild pitch. Not bad for someone who was too slow to play on the offensive line at Penn State.

Scioscia reached the big leagues for good in 1981, but still split time with veteran catcher Steve Yeager. Even though Scioscia was still only 22 years old, he was behind the plate most of the time when the Dodgers' newest phenom Fernando Valenzuela was on the mound. Fernando, who was said to be just 20 at the time, spawned "Fernandomania," which took on a life of its own. Fernando began the season with eight consecutive victories. He finished the season with a 13-7 record and a 2.48 ERA and had a league-leading eight shutouts. But Fernando was more than his numbers.

"The whole experience was a bunch of things coming together at the right time," Scioscia said. "He was an incredible talent and he was pitching in a city that was just waiting for someone like him to come out of Mexico. It was exciting for all of Southern California, not just the Mexican community. I was just 22 and he was 20…it was a unique experience."

That 1981 season was more than just Fernando. It was a Dodger team that was nearing a transition phase, but still had their core group of players like Yeager, Steve Garvey, Davey Lopes, Bill Russell, Ron Cey and Dusty Baker. It was a team that failed to win the World Series in matchups against the Yankees in 1977 and '78, but in 1981 it broke through with a World Series victory over those same Yankees. Yeager, Cey and Pedro Guerrero were named co-MVPs of the Series.

"The '81 team was the best team I ever played on," Scioscia says.

Scioscia took over the primary catching duties in 1982, but he tore the rotator cuff in his right shoulder in 1983 and played in only 12 games, watching as the Dodgers reached the playoffs before being eliminated by his hometown Philadelphia Phillies.

Scioscia returned to play the 1984 season, and in 1985 the Dodgers were back in the playoffs. They lost in the National League playoffs to the St. Louis Cardinals, but these Dodgers had represented the organization's next stage.

"The '85 team was a different team, a younger team," Scioscia said. "It was a transition team, a different team from the teams of the '70's. It wasn't Garvey, Lopes, Russell and Cey anymore. It was Greg Brock, Mike Marshall, Fernando, Steve Sax and Bobby Welch. Orel Hershiser pitched for us that year. The team was a product of the Dodger farm system. It had carried over."

The Dodgers had a playoff drought in 1986 and '87, but found magic in 1988. They were sparked by Orel Hershiser's incredible performance throughout the regular season and the playoffs, and got one of the most memorable home runs in baseball history from Kirk Gibson in Game 1 of the World Series against the Oakland A's.

But if not for an earlier home run by Scioscia, Gibson's homer might not have ever occurred. Scioscia's ninth-inning home run off Dwight "Doc" Gooden in Game 4 of the National League Championship Series helped lift the Dodgers to the National League pennant over the heavily-favored New York Mets. That victory gave Gibson and Hershiser the opportunity for their World Series heroics, and the Dodgers had their second World Series championship of the decade.

That season, Hershiser put together one of the most impressive seasons by a pitcher in major league history. He won 23 games, broke the major league record for consecutive scoreless innings (59), and Scioscia was with him every step of the way.

Scioscia, however, was not there when Hershiser recorded the final out against the A's to win the World Series. Instead, it was backup catcher Rick Dempsey who was pictured on the cover of Sports Illustrated, lifting a triumphant Hershiser into the air. One game earlier, Scioscia hurt his knee trying to break up a double play at second base. He didn't play in the deciding Game 5.

"Not having him catch the last game of the World Series was devastating to me," Hershiser said. "I love Rick Dempsey, but I know every time Mike sees the cover he thinks it should have been him. He was hustling from first to second got hurt. It was crushing."

Scioscia got over it. He was named to the National League All-Star team in both 1989 and '90. He played for the Dodgers in 1991 and '92, but after years of getting beat up behind the plate, his playing career was nearing an end. Scioscia tried to continue his career with both the San Diego Padres and Texas Rangers in 1993 and '94, but another rotator cuff injury in the spring of 1993 was too much to overcome and his playing career was finished.

"It was definitely a transition, but one thing that made it easier was playing that long and giving myself every opportunity."

INTO THE DUGOUT

Though his body would not cooperate and allow him to continue his playing career, Scioscia's mind held a wealth of information that made him a natural for a coaching career. And there was no better way for him to pay back all that he learned in the Dodger organization than to pass it on to future Dodger stars. When it became evident that his playing career was nearing an end, Scioscia began thinking about a coaching career.

Scioscia rejoined the Dodgers in 1995 as the organization's minor league catching coordinator and held that job through the 1996 season. He joined Dodger manager Bill Russell's staff in 1997 as the club's bench coach, and after the season got his first managerial experience, managing the Peoria Javelinas in the Arizona Fall League.

He returned as the Dodgers' bench coach in 1998, but the Dodgers were about make big changes and Scioscia would not be a part of it. When Rupert Murdoch and his Fox Group's purchase of the Dodgers from the O'Malley family became official in 1998, change took place quickly.

Manager Bill Russell and general manager Fred Claire were fired in June of 1998 and replaced on an interim basis by Glenn Hoffman and Lasorda, respectively. After the season, Scioscia watched as the club hired Kevin Malone to be the club's general manager. But Malone never considered Scioscia as the club's next manager, deciding to go outside the organization and hiring Davey Johnson. It was then that Scioscia knew he had to make some decisions of his own.

"That's when I knew I needed to take steps in order to become a major league manager," Scioscia said.

Scioscia was given the job as the club's manager at Class-AAA Albuquerque, but it would be his final year with the organization. Immediately after the season, Scioscia met with Malone.

"I was wondering where the organization was going, if they could give me an idea," Scioscia said. "He said there were so many things in transition that they weren't clear. I thought the best thing for me was to get out early and give myself the opportunity to look for some spots."

Just like that, Scioscia was an ex-Dodger in every sense of the word. He had previously turned down opportunities to interview for managerial openings with the Tampa Bay Devil Rays and Chicago White Sox, but there would be another opportunity yet to come.

Scioscia had talked to Bill Bavasi before Bavasi resigned as the Angels' general manager late in 1999. But once Bavasi was gone, Scioscia could only sit and wait to see who would become the next general manager of the Angels.

At the time, former Yankees GM Bob Watson appeared to be the frontrunner, and he was expected to hire one of his former teammates with the Yankees, either Willie Randolph of Chris Chambliss. But Angels president Tony Tavares surprised everybody with his hiring of Bill Stoneman, who had been with the Montreal Expos and was known more for his financial wizardry than running a baseball team.

Once Stoneman was in, managerial candidates like Don Baylor and Phil Garner had already signed on with other teams. Scioscia got in touch with Stoneman and landed an interview. Little did Scioscia know, he got help from another ex-Dodger.

"Bill Stoneman called me before he hired Mike," said Claire, the ex-Dodgers GM. "We talked for 45 minutes to an hour, and I told Bill, if you hire Mike it will be a great decision for your organization. He will be a successful manager. He was respected as a player and coach, he's well prepared and he's dedicated. He does everything he possibly can."

Scioscia was asked back for a second interview, at which time he was hired as the Angels manager. Three years later, Scioscia's Angels won the World Series and he was named the American League manager of the year.

Success, though, would not shake Scioscia's foundation. It never has. His wife Anne first introduced herself to Scioscia by offering him chocolate chip cookies she baked. Their children, Matthew and Taylor, come first in the Scioscias' lives.

When the Baseball Writers Association of America tried to contact Scioscia to tell him he won the manager of the year award, he wasn't home. He finally was reached via cell phone at a botanical garden. He was on a field trip with Taylor's fifth-grade class.

"I'm learning a lot about botany," Scioscia quipped with glee.

And he meant it.

Troy Percival got the save in Game 7 of the World Series, but not before
getting into a war of words with ex-Angel Mo Vaughn.

3

Mo here, Mo Gaughn

Scioscia likely never would have become the Angels manager if not for the club's implosion in 1999. Prior to the 1997 season, the Angels hired ex-Astros manager and Dodger minor leaguer Terry Collins to be their manager. General manager Bill Bavasi and club president Tony Tavares liked Collins' no-nonsense approach, which they thought was just what the players needed after time under the more laid-back Marcel Lachemann.

The Angels played relatively well under Collins, even if it wasn't good enough to reach the playoffs. They went 84-78 in 1997 and 85-77 in 1998, contending for a playoff spot both seasons. The Angels were close, many thought, and simply needed that final piece of the puzzle to win in 1999. Bavasi was given the opportunity from ownership to get that piece. He courted pitcher Randy Johnson, who eventually decided to sign with the Arizona Diamondbacks.

But Bavasi landed his other target, Red Sox first baseman Mo Vaughn. Bavasi impressed Vaughn with a letter, imploring Vaughn to pick up his East Coast roots and move west. And it didn't hurt that Bavasi offered Vaughn $80 million over six years. Vaughn signed with the Angels, who believed they were in position to get over the top and reach the playoffs for the first time since 1986.

On opening night in 1999 a sellout crowd came to Anaheim's Edison Field to see Vaughn and the Angels play the Cleveland Indians. But in the top of the first inning, the second batter of the game, Omar Vizquel, hit a foul popup near the Indians' first-base dugout. Vaughn drifted over near the dugout, looking into the sky, then fell into the dugout, landing hard on his left ankle.

Vaughn shook it off and stayed in the game. But when he fell while batting later in the game, it was obvious the injury was worse than first imagined. Vaughn came out of the game and was diagnosed with a severe high-ankle sprain.

Ironically, there had been a short fence at the top of the dugout steps to protect players in the dugout from foul line drives and to keep defensive players from falling into the dugout like Vaughn did. But Collins had the fences removed after the 1998 season because he had trouble seeing the field as clearly as he wanted to. Soon after Vaughn's injury, the fences returned.

But the damage had been done, and not only to Vaughn's ankle. A season that began with so much promise started on the wrong foot and only got worse. Even though Vaughn returned and led the team with 33 homers and 108 RBIs while playing with a noticeable limp, the tone had been set. The team went 70-92, but reached a boiling point late in August that led to major changes to the organization.

THE FIGHT

Even during a bad season the Angels had their good moments, and seemed to be having one on Aug. 31, 1999 against the Cleveland Indians. The Angels led, 12-4, going into the bottom of the eighth when the Indians put together a 10-run rally, the final runs coming home on a Richie Sexson home run off Angels closer Troy Percival.

After Sexson's homer, David Justice stepped into the batter's box and was hit by a pitch from Percival. Justice charged the mound, throwing his helmet at Percival before reaching him. Both dugouts emptied and the fight ensued.

After the game the team was in the clubhouse and saw the highlights of the game and fight on television. During the chaos, Vaughn was shown still in the dugout, and many Angels players noticed. Percival in particular was angered and confronted Vaughn. Vaughn's response was that as the designated hitter, he was in the clubhouse when the fight began. And by the time he reached the dugout all the action on the field subsided.

That answer apparently wasn't enough for some of Vaughn's teammates. On the following day, several Angels players met with Collins and stated they weren't going to play that day if Vaughn was in the lineup. Collins, feeling he had no other option, benched Vaughn that day.

A week later, Collins tearfully announced his resignation. Later that month, Bavasi also resigned rather than heed the advice of upper management and tear apart the foundation of the club that he helped build. Ironically the next general manager, Bill Stoneman, felt the same way and kept the core players intact.

SCIOSCIA TAKES CONTROL

Upon his hiring, Scioscia immediately had an impact with the organization, revamping the coaching staff by bringing in fellow ex-Dodgers like hitting coach Mickey Hatcher, first base coach Alfredo Griffin and third base coach Ron Roenicke. Scioscia also would have considered Orel Hershiser to be his pitching coach, but Hershiser was still pitching in the big leagues.

Instead, Stoneman and Scioscia agreed on Bud Black, who was working in the Cleveland Indians' front office. Scioscia's bench coach would be the only remaining link to past Angels coaching regimes, Joe Maddon. Maddon was Scioscia's link to the Angels' players past. He had been with the organization since 1981 as a minor league coach and manager and nobody knew the Angels players better.

Maddon was also the club's resident intellect, bringing the use of computerized breakdowns of pitcher/batter matchups and defensive alignments to a new level.

Soon after spring training for the 2000 season began, there was a new optimism in the clubhouse. While there still might have been some friction between Vaughn and some of his teammates, it was put on the backburner for the good of the team. And Vaughn, amid off-season reports he would be traded, insisted he was happy to be back.

"I read all this about me wanting to get traded," Vaughn said at the outset of spring training. "First of all, nothing I've ever started did I not finish. I'm not about to jump ship when things don't go the way they're supposed to go. I will always believe my choice to come here was the right choice. This organization took care of me, gave me an opportunity. Things don't always happen right away. Last year was a bad year but we're in a different situation now."

With a new coaching staff in place and apparent harmony in the clubhouse, Scioscia was left to make believers out of his players. It was a team full of talented players, but players who had not been able to reach the playoffs despite coming so close in recent seasons.

Even lifelong Angel Tim Salmon had questioned the team's direction following the 1999 season, but he changed his tune after a few days in Camp Scioscia. "This is the first day toward redemption," he said. "I was talking to some of the coaches and trainers and they were saying 'Man, what a different attitude there is in there (clubhouse).' This is a fresh start."

ANGELS IN THE OUTFIELD

One of Scioscia's spring training priorities was to figure out a way to fit four starting outfielders into a lineup that had room for only three. Salmon, Garret Anderson, Darin Erstad and Jim Edmonds were all legitimate starters, but Scioscia had to balance putting one in the designated hitter spot or even on the bench for any particular game without hurting any egos are causing dissention.

Edmonds and Anderson were entering the final season of their respective contracts and one of them figured to go. The New York Yankees emerged as the team most interested in one of the Angels outfielders, and they targeted Darin Erstad. However, they soon found out that Erstad wasn't going anywhere, and soon turned their attention to Edmonds.

Edmonds' career with the Angels had been mixed with incredible displays of talent and maddening frustration from those who believed Edmonds wasn't reaching the potential of his immense talent. Anderson, meanwhile, was soft-spoken and consistent as anyone in the league. Eventually, Edmonds could not escape hearing the rumors and it seemed to distract him. "Everyone says I'm going to be traded, but the front office says I'm not," Edmonds said. "Who do you believe?"

Getting word that Edmonds seemed to be distracted by the rumors, Stoneman approached Edmonds and told him what was going on. Edmonds seemed satisfied by Stoneman's words, but Stoneman never guaranteed Edmonds would not be traded. Less than a week later, Edmonds was traded not to the Yankees, but to the St. Louis Cardinals for pitcher Kent Bottenfield, who had won 18 games and was an All-Star the previous season, and young second baseman Adam Kennedy, who found himself behind Cardinals starter Fernando Vina.

A couple days after the trade Edmonds returned to the Angels' spring training complex in Tempe, Ariz. to gather his things and say his goodbyes.

Edmonds walked into the clubhouse at 10 a.m. with the team already on the field. He peeked out the clubhouse door and looked at his former teammates before sitting down to talk to a reporter. A few players came in, one at a time, and wished him well. But when Anderson came in, the two hugged, and Edmonds began to cry. "It's like moving away from your family," Edmonds said. "How do you react? It's hard to talk about."

When Edmonds was told that former teammates Gary DiSarcina and Tim Salmon reminisced about playing with Edmonds in the minors, Edmonds' eyes welled up with tears. He spent 12 years in the organization, and grew up only a few miles from the Anaheim Stadium.

Angels players were disappointed to see a player of Edmonds' talent leave, but it also settled a potentially disruptive situation before the season began. "Now there's no rotation in the outfield, and the DH situation is settled," DiSarcina said. "Guys can come to the ballpark knowing where they're playing. Darin (Erstad) does not want to be a DH; he's 27 years old. It puts people in roles, and that's good for chemistry."

2000 SEASON

Even without Edmonds, the Angels knew they would have plenty of offense in 2000. With a healthy Vaughn surrounded by proven hitters like Salmon and Anderson, the expected emergence of Troy Glaus and a bounce-back year from Erstad, they were going to score runs. The acquisition of Bottenfield was expected to give the beleaguered pitching staff a boost, especially since veterans like Ken Hill and Tim Belcher would have trouble staying healthy and productive.

The Angels finished April a mediocre 13-13, but were only 1.5 games out of first place in the A.L. West. After May, they were 27-26 and cluttered with the rest of the division only one-half game out of first. By the end of June, the Angels were still treading water at 41-38, but fell five games out of first place.

By this time though, one thing had become quite clear. Erstad, who dropped to .253 with 13 homers in 1999, was putting together a remarkable season. Feeling comfortable in the leadoff spot and staying healthy, Erstad had 100 hits by June 10, the fastest any player had gotten there since 1934 when Heinie Manush of the Washington Senators did it in 60 games.

At season's end, Erstad had batted .355 with a major league-leading 240 hits, 25 homers, 100 RBIs, 121 runs scored and 28 stolen bases, arguably the best offensive performance by a leadoff hitter in major league history. He became the only player in major league history to drive in 100 runs from the leadoff spot.

The Angels offense followed suit, setting numerous club records, including most hits, home runs and RBIs. Anderson, Glaus, Salmon and Vaughn combined to become the first foursome in American League history to hit at least 30 home runs. The Toronto Blue Jays matched the Angels' feat the same season.

The pitching, though, was a different matter. Before the season Stoneman had decided not to keep the club's all-time winningest pitcher—Chuck Finley—for financial reasons, but they could have used his arm. Because of numerous injuries to the pitching staff, Scioscia had 16 different pitchers start games in 2000, a club record they could have done without.

Even so, the Angels finished August still in it, only four games out even though they still had a mediocre record of 68-65. However, they began September with a five-game losing streak, fell seven games out and never recovered. Both Seattle and Oakland took off in September and both made the playoffs, Oakland as the division winner and Seattle the wild card. The Angels finished 82-80, 9 1/2 games out but much better off under new regime headed by Stoneman and Scioscia.

2001 SEASON

Vaughn played through the end of the 2000 season with soreness in his left biceps muscle but was diagnosed with nothing more than tendonitis. He went into the off-season like any other, prepared to work out and get stronger for the next season. But sometime around the New Year, Vaughn felt something pop in his arm while working out.

Vaughn was diagnosed with a ruptured biceps tendon, the tendon that connects the muscle to the joint. Surgery was needed Vaughn would be lost for the season. Nobody knew it at the time, but Vaughn had played his last game as an Angel.

Scioscia, though, was confident the club's offense could be just as good without Vaughn. Not that they had any one player to take Vaughn's place, but that as a group they could make up the difference. In the meantime, Vaughn focused on his rehabilitation from surgery, but seeing his teammates often wasn't in the cards. "I don't want to lose touch with them," Vaughn said early in spring training. "But also I don't want to have the team see me like that. I don't want them to think about what happened to me, they need to focus on what they have to do. This team has had enough negativity."

In an effort to replace the 36 homers and 117 RBIs provided by Vaughn in 2000, the club signed Jose Canseco to be the DH and Wally Joyner to compete for playing time at first base. Canseco played in spring training "not to get hurt," but Scioscia and the coaches saw it as a lack of hustle. Canseco was cut before the end of spring training.

As Canseco was going out the door, Glenallen Hill came in. Hill, though, didn't last long either. He was hitting .136 when the Angels released him on June 1st. Joyner also didn't make it through the season, retiring on June 16th.

Pat Rapp and Ismael Valdes were signed to fill out the starting rotation, but they were inexpensive fill-ins that didn't pan out. The offense, without Vaughn and with sub-par seasons from Tim Salmon and Darin Erstad, the Angels struggled to gain any positive momentum.

Though they battled through more mediocrity early in the season and had no chance of catching the Seattle Mariners, who were on their way to 116 victories, the Angels remained in the race for a wild-card berth. On Aug. 19, they beat the Indians to go a season-best eight games over .500 at 66-58 and were five games behind the Oakland A's in the wild-card standings.

But the club fell apart after that, losing 29 of its final 38 games, including 19 of its final 21. The Angels finished 75-87, a step back from the club's first season under Scioscia. It was back to the drawing board.

THE RADIO INTERVIEW

The Angels went into the winter after the 2001 season believing they would be better, simply by getting the offensive production from a healthy Vaughn they missed in 2001. But in December, Vaughn was interviewed on a Boston radio station and said he'd like to return to the Red Sox.

That irked the Angels, who were eager to trade him and rid themselves of the $48 million that remained on Vaughn's contract. But figuring there would be few teams, if any, interested in taking on that kind of money and taking a player coming off a serious injury who also had weight issues was a long shot.

Vaughn also had a limited no-trade clause. Vaughn and the Angels each could pick three teams to which Vaughn could be traded. A trade to any other team would require Vaughn's approval. Vaughn picked the Yankees, Red Sox and Mets; the Angels picked the Dodgers, Orioles and Braves.

Stoneman admitted he did not have high hopes of trading Vaughn, but negotiations with the Mets resulted in a Dec. 27 trade for pitcher Kevin Appier, a proven and established starting pitcher that could help bolster the starting rotation. Though the Angels didn't gain much financially (Appier still had $32 million remaining on his contract), they got much-needed pitching help and avoided a potential problem in the clubhouse after Vaughn's comments in the radio interview.

His three years with the club were filled with injuries, disappointment and controversy, and he got paid $40 million by the club. He never fully fit in with the team or with the lifestyle on the West Coast. Mo Vaughn was Gaughn, if not forgotten.

When Scott Spiezio wasn't coming up with key hits for the Angels, he was writing songs for his band.

4

The Start of Something Big

The trade of Mo Vaughn for pitcher Kevin Appier was not the only significant off-season move the Angels made in preparation for the 2002 season. Only one day before the Vaughn-Appier trade, Stoneman signed free-agent pitcher Aaron Sele to a three-year contract worth $24 million.

Sele had won 17 and 15 games, respectively, in the previous two seasons with the Seattle Mariners, who had no interest in re-signing him. That might have seemed a little odd, especially considering Sele won 19 games and 18 games in his two seasons with the Texas Rangers in the two years before that.

Sele was criticized in those cities for not being able to win big games, going 0-6 in playoff games. And there were rumors that there might have been problems with Sele's right (throwing) shoulder. Nevertheless, the Angels figured if they could get the regular-season production out of Sele he had achieved in the previous four years, he'd be worth it. With Appier also on board, the Angels had an upgrade in the starting rotation from the previous season, having replaced Ismael Valdes and Pat Rapp.

There was one final piece the Angels needed, and that was a designated hitter. In 2001 they Angels experimented and failed with Jose Canseco, Glenallen Hill and many others. By season's end, the Angels had used 15 different players and got only eight home runs in the DH spot. They needed an upgrade there, and they got it when they found the Toronto Blue Jays in the process of dumping salary.

The Angels acquired Brad Fullmer, who had averaged 25 home runs in the previous two seasons, for minor league pitcher Brian Cooper. Spring training was set to begin, and for the first time in many years, the Angels seemed to be settled.

"I think we're much more well-rounded than in years past," right fielder Tim Salmon said. "Every team has areas to fill going into the off-season, but not every team is able to do it. We did."

With another year of development under the belts of starting pitchers Jarrod Washburn, Ramon Ortiz and Scott Schoeneweis, and the expected return to normalcy of Salmon and Darin Erstad, who both slumped in 2001, the Angels felt confident. And that confidence exuded from the top.

"We've taken huge steps forward in important areas," said Scioscia, who was about to start his third season with the club. "The starting rotation, and not just Kevin Appier and Aaron Sele, but also the development of the three younger guys. They're developing at a pace where they've made footsteps in the major leagues and they're ready to take off from there. And the offense. Even though the names are the same in some areas, they're better just with experience."

PERCIVAL VS. VAUGHN, ROUND 2

Just when it appeared the Angels would have a nice quiet spring, a reporter asked closer Troy Percival how the Angels would make up for the loss in leadership previously provided by Mo Vaughn. Percival scoffed at the notion the Angels would miss the leadership of someone who had not been around.

"We may miss Mo's bat, but we won't miss his leadership," Percival said, noting Vaughn rarely came around the team as he rehabilitated from surgery on his left arm. "Darin Erstad is our leader."

In Percival's mind, the comments weren't a slap at Vaughn, simply a statement of fact. They could not miss something they didn't have. But when a reporter picked up Percival's comments and relayed them to Vaughn, now in Port St. Lucie, Fla. in spring training with the Mets, the first baseman reacted angrily.

"Who the (expletive) is Troy Percival?" Vaughn said. "What has he done in this game? Has he led his team to a pennant? Has he ever (expletive) pitched in a big game that meant something?…He hasn't done (expletive) to lead them anywhere. I got hardware, I got playoff appearances. I got an MVP. I've been to the playoffs twice. What the hell has he done? Who the hell is he?"

About the Angels, Vaughn said: "I tried to be cool here. I tried to be nice of this whole situation concerning the Angels all the way around. Ain't none of them done a damn thing in the damn game, bottom line. They ain't got no flags hanging at (expletive) Edison Field, so the hell with them."

Predictably, reporters went back to Percival for his reaction to Vaughn's comments, looking for another slam in this cross-country tennis match. But it didn't happen. Percival took the high road and ended the controversy right there.

"What I said and what I'll continue to say is that last year we missed his bat," Percival said. "But you ask 25 guys in here and they'll tell you the same thing:

Darin Erstad is the leader of our team. Did Mo Vaughn lead our team last year? No, he wasn't here. You can't miss somebody that wasn't here."

Percival also said he had no problems with Vaughn's comments about never playing in the postseason.

"You know what? You take out all the expletives, and he's right," Percival said. "How many times have I been to the playoffs? How many times have I won? It's not an individual game. I don't play it that way....I don't live in the past. We don't have a lot of pennants. We don't have a lot of World Series. But I came back here because the future of this team looks bright. That's why I'm here."

Still, Vaughn remained hot on the other side of the country, blaming the Angels for not diagnosing the injury soon enough. "That organization frickin' destroyed my arm," Vaughn said in reference to the surgery he had to repair a torn biceps tendon. Vaughn felt pain toward the end of the 2000 season in his arm, but played out the year. It was discovered later he needed surgery.

But ever the level-headed one, Scioscia cooled the situation.

"I've never had any conversations with Mo that would say he couldn't go out and play," Scioscia said. "He wanted to go out and play, and he did well. Mo's a gamer. His rehab didn't go smoothly, but that's not unique to rehab. Mo's injuries were probably the toughest things he went through out here. It was tough for him to assume a leadership role. That's a fact, I don't think it's a slam at Mo. We wish Mo well. There are no hard feelings."

And with that, the Mo Vaughn era was officially over.

THE HAYMAKER

Arizona's Cactus League games started out like any other year in spring training for the Angels, with the starting pitchers getting their work in, and the position players building up stamina and finding their rhythm and timing at the plate. The intensity level at the games is not high, and it carries over into the seats. The fans at spring training games in Arizona are there to catch some rays as much as catch a foul ball.

But the serenity of spring was rudely shattered one afternoon at Tempe Diablo Stadium when the Angels and Padres took the field and quickly engaged in two bench—and bullpen-clearing fights.

The first fight took place in the top of the first inning when with two out and nobody on base, Angels pitcher Aaron Sele hit the Padres Ryan Klesko in the back on the first pitch. Klesko immediately charged the mound and fought with Sele as players from both teams piled on.

Klesko was ejected but jawed with Scioscia before leaving the field. Sele had to go to the trainer's room because his contact lenses had popped out. He returned to the mound and gave up a two-run homer to Phil Nevin before getting out of the inning.

Then in the bottom of the first, the Angels had a runner on first with one out when Padres pitcher Bobby Jones threw a fastball inside to Troy Glaus, who glared back at Jones. After a called strike, Jones threw the next pitch high and tight, Glaus hitting the dirt to avoid the pitch. He immediately got up and charged Jones, but was tackled by catcher Adan Amezcua before reaching Jones.

Klesko ran back onto the field in street clothes, but didn't fight. An enraged Scott Spiezio, though, did. Spiezio, who started the game at third base for the Angels, threw punches at Padres coach Tim Flannery and manager Bruce Bochy, connecting when he swung at Flannery. Angels hitting coach Mickey Hatcher emerged with a cut under his right eye. Spiezio, Jones, Nevin and Glaus were thrown out after the second fight.

Why such temper in a spring training game? According to Klesko, Sele was upset with him after hitting a home run against Sele in an interleague game in 2001 when Sele was with the Mariners. It wasn't the home run that upset Sele, but how Klesko appeared to pose, freezing at the end of his follow-through.

"(Sele) told Nevin if he saw me again he would hit me," Klesko said. "We kind of knew it was coming. It's obvious, it's the first pitch, the first time I've seen him (since). He hits me in the back, what am I supposed to do? Go to first?"

However, Sele denied there was any bad blood between the two.

"It sounds like a long theory," Sele said. "I was trying to throw hard, in. If he thought I was throwing at him, he did the right thing (by charging). I have absolutely no problem with somebody trying to protect himself."

The pitches that nearly hit Glaus, though, incensed many of the Angels, particularly Spiezio.

"Throwing at a guy's head is off limits," Spiezio said. "It should have been taken care of when Klesko went out there, then they throw at Glaus' head? What was that crap? The first fight was more of a reaction, the second one, I was angry."

Nevin, a former Angel, said he had no problem with the actions of Sele, Klesko, Jones or Glaus, but Spiezio's actions wouldn't be forgotten.

"Fights happen, but when guys come in throwing cheap shots, they need to be taught a lesson," Nevin said. "And there are a couple guys over there that need to be taught a lesson."

After the field was cleared following the second fight, Spiezio made one last trip to the field to talk to plate umpire Brian Gorman.

"There was something I wanted to clear up," Spiezio said. "Bruce Bochy said I was kicking guys in the first melee, and that wasn't the case at all. I told the umps, watch the tapes, I'd never do something like that."

After an investigation by Bob Watson, Major League Baseball's vice president in charge of discipline, Spiezio was hit with a six-game suspension that would be enforced beginning on opening day. Spiezio entered camp expecting to get most of the starts at first base in place of the departed Vaughn, sharing time with Shawn Wooten.

But Wooten tore a ligament in his thumb during spring training and would be out until July. So the Angels' opening day first baseman was utility player Benji Gil. Spiezio, though, would be back. And in a big way.

MAN WITH A BAND

Catch Scott Spiezio away from the ballpark and one would hardly imagine he was a major leaguer. Some might say he's too friendly. Others yet might say he belongs on stage. And in fact, he is.

On road trips during the baseball season, Spiezio often stays up all night writing music and lyrics for his rock band, Sandfrog.

"My main focus is baseball, it always will be," Spiezio said. "My love for baseball outweighs music by far. But one thing music does is it keeps my mind consistent. If I had a great game I don't gloat about it and if I had a bad game I don't worry about it. When I get to my hotel room and write until 5 in the morning, it doesn't allow me to dwell on that night's game.

"That's one reason I bought a guitar, to get myself into a consistent mindset."

Spiezio is as mild-mannered as they come, so don't be fooled by his music. He says the term for his music these days is "Nu metal," which is heavy metal tuned down a notch.

"Our older stuff did sound like Black Sabbath and Alice in Chains," Spiezio said.

Sandfrog usually played in Spiezio's hometown of Morris, Ill. where some of his bandmates lived. During the baseball season the band waited for Spiezio to come up with the new material and they got to work during the off-season. Mostly, the band's more-experienced musicians "tweaked" Spiezio's material to clean it up.

This isn't your typical wannabe heavy-metal band. In fact, one of the band's members developed its website, Sandfrog.com, complete with videos of the band's recent gigs.

It's doubtful, though, that Spiezio's father, Ed, pushed him into music. Ed Spiezio played third base and the outfield from 1964-72 with the Cardinals, Padres and White Sox.

He didn't get to play much with the Cardinals, who had Ken Boyer at third and Lou Brock and Curt Flood in the outfield. But he was taken by the Padres in the 1969 expansion draft and became their starting third baseman.

Preston Gomez, a special assistant to Angels' general manager Bill Stoneman, was the Padres' manager at the time.

"He hit the first home run in Padres history," Gomez recalled. "He had some power, but his son has more power. He's really a nice guy, a very high-class man. Just like his son."

Ed Spiezio played his final major league game Sept. 20, 1972, one day before Scott was born. Ed still had some baseball left in him, but figured he needed be home for his family. And besides, he could make more money running the family's furniture store in Morris than he could playing baseball. Ed still runs the same furniture store.

Meanwhile, Scott turned out to be just like dad, more or less. The younger Spiezio was versatile, able to play first, third and the outfield. He played a full season with the A's at second base.

But it was his versatility that contributed to the utility-player tag he tried to shed. When the Angels traded Vaughn to the Mets during the off-season, Spiezio had his chance. And in 2002, he would make the most of it.

BREAKING CAMP

Even though the Angels had considerable confidence in themselves, they weren't given much of a chance outside of their own clubhouse. Just about any publication had them finishing behind the Mariners and A's in the A.L. West, and many had them finishing behind the Texas Rangers, even though it was the Rangers who had finished in last place in 2001.

It wasn't a position unfamiliar to the Angels. They were used to be overlooked, and their history of failures had as much to do with it as anything. But it was a position that helped the Angels grab onto an approach of "Us against the world." Starting in spring training, they seemed able to block out any and all distractions.

"Being an underdog is nice," Salmon said. "But I'd be willing to bet you teams in our division don't think of us as an afterthought."

No matter what other teams thought of the Angels, as a successful and relatively quiet spring training came to an end, the Angels left Arizona confident, healthy and ready to begin the 2002 season.

After a sluggish April, the Angels got hot in May and were sparked by
their intense center fielder, Darin Erstad.

5

One Day at a Time

Scioscia preached it until he was blue in the face: There was no game more important than that day's game. And when it was over, no matter how difficult a loss it might have been, it was over. The focus would go to the next game.

And so it went. Scioscia would not allow his players to get ahead of themselves. He would not allow his players to concern themselves with how other teams in the league were doing. "We're only concerned about in-house," Scioscia said over and over and over again.

It turned about to be a necessary philosophy early in the 2002 season. The Angels played the Cleveland Indians in the Major Leagues' season-opener. In front of a sellout crowd and a national television audience, the Angels were shut out by the Indians and pitcher Bartolo Colon, 6-0.

The Angels won three of their next four to go 3-2, but braced to begin a nine-game homestand against their American League West foes, the Seattle Mariners, Oakland A's and Texas Rangers. The Angels lost four in a row to Seattle, then the next to two Oakland. The season was barely two weeks old, and already the Angels had a six-game losing streak and were 3-8.

They continued to flounder deeper into April, and after a 1-0 loss to the Mariners on April 23, the Angels were 6-14, the worst record in franchise history through 20 games. Even worse for the Angels was they were already 10 1/2 games behind Seattle in the division, and falling behind so far so quickly was the last thing they wanted after finishing 2001 a club-record 41 games out.

By that time, other teams were losing patience with their managers and firing them. Milwaukee's Davey Lopes, Detroit's Phil Garner, Kansas City's Tony Muser and Colorado's Buddy Bell had been fired. Was Scioscia next to go?

Angels general manager Bill Stoneman said he never considered it. Scioscia said he never worried about it.

"I'm ultimately accountable," Scioscia said. "That's the way baseball is, the manager is accountable. But I haven't even thought about that scenario. And it absolutely won't change what I do on a day-to-day basis."

Scioscia was not only getting public support from Stoneman, but also his players.

"I don't think he deserves any of the blame," first baseman Scott Spiezio said. "He's not out there playing. It's not like players are clashing with him. He gets along with all the players and coaches. There's no hostility between him and the players."

Scioscia was in the third and final year of his initial contract with the team, which was to pay him a total of $1 million over three seasons. But he signed a contract extension in 2001 that put him under contract through 2005, with a club option for 2006. That contract called for an average annual salary of about $1 million per season.

"He's been very positive and supportive," Spiezio said. "He does nothing but tell us how he believes in us. As a player he went through tough times just like anybody, so he knows how to get out of it. The fault right now is on the players."

It didn't take long for the Angels to climb out of their hole. Sitting at 6-14, they immediately went on an eight-game winning streak to even their season record at 14-14. They cut their deficit in the division to 5 1/2 games. Any confidence that might have been shaken returned. Four days after their eight-game winning streak ended, they started another streak. Again, they won eight in a row and improved to 23-16.

Along the way, the club gave to its fans things they would never forget. Tops on the list was the sight of shortstop David Eckstein, listed in the media guide as 5-foot-8 but who readily admits he's 5-6 1/2, hitting a grand slam on April 27.

It's not that Eckstein isn't strong enough to hit a home run, although it's mandatory that he pull the ball down the line to get it over the fence. It's more that Eckstein knows his role with the club better than anyone. His job as a hitter is to be a pest, get on base any way he can. He wants to hit the ball on the ground, not in the air.

So while the grand slam wasn't expected, it wasn't totally surprising. What was surprising was that Eckstein hit another grand slam the very next day, on April 28. That one, though, ended the game and gave the Angels an 8-5 victory over the shell-shocked Toronto Blue Jays, the victim of both grand slams.

Incredibly, Eckstein hit his third grand slam of the season on June 9, and led the majors in grand slams by the time the season was finished. Unusual? Improbable? Maybe. But with Eckstein around, it was easy to believe anything was possible. Angels closer Troy Percival was asked during the playoffs when he thought 2002 might be the Angels' year. "When Eck hit those grand slams back-to-back, I knew anything was possible," Percival said.

THE ECK FACTOR

Eckstein won't deny his small stature put him in some humorous situations as he worked his way up to the major leagues. But he scoffs if one suggests it has been an obstacle.

"It's never prevented me from getting an opportunity," said the native of Sanford, Fla. "And that's all you can ask for."

Eckstein laughs about the time he was asked for his identification by a minor league general manager when he reported one year. And he shrugs when talking about the time he was mistaken for a clubhouse attendant when he was in his first major league spring training, in 2000 with the Boston Red Sox.

Eckstein has faced potentially bigger road blocks. Eckstein's younger sister Susan suffered kidney failure as a teen-ager and needed a transplant. Mother Patricia gave Susan one of hers.

"When we found out what happened to Susan, we (Eckstein, his two brothers and another sister) got tested," Eckstein said. "The day we brought Susan home from the transplant, the phone rang. They said Kenny and Christine were in the process of losing a kidney. They both had about 30 percent function."

Eckstein and his other brother Ricky were fine, but they continue to undergo periodic testing.

Both Kenny and Christine underwent dialysis for two years before donors were found for both in the same week. All three—Kenny, Christine and Susan—are doing well.

Other than that, Eckstein grew up in a normal family environment. He was an active kid, but once he got to high school baseball became his focus.

"They wanted me to play basketball," he said. "But my dad (Whitey) said I should concentrate on one sport. Basketball overlapped with baseball, and besides, look at me."

No, there usually isn't much of a future for basketball players who have to jump to flip a light switch. Then again, it seems Eckstein would have found a way to succeed.

Eckstein was ticketed to be the second baseman at the Angels' Class-AAA team in Salt Lake City, Utah, going into his first spring training with the Angels in 2001. But an injury to second baseman Adam Kennedy during camp opened up a roster spot and Eckstein never gave it up.

What was the Angels' gain was the Boston Red Sox's loss. Eckstein was drafted by the Red Sox in 1997 and played in their minor league system until August of 2000 when the Red Sox needed a spot on their 40-man roster. They figured they could put Eckstein on waivers, and when no team claimed him, they could keep him, returning him to Class-AAA Pawtucket.

Angels general manager Bill Stoneman, though, took the advice of his scouts and claimed Eckstein. It was an unusual move to make, considering Eckstein's size.

"It didn't keep us from taking a chance," Stoneman said. "But I would venture to say it would keep other teams from taking a chance. Scouts today are looking for the biggest, fastest, strongest guys. But one thing we talk to our scouts about is heart, how he plays with the tools he has. It showed up in our reports and it showed up when he arrived in spring training.

"When you make a move, you don't know how it's going to turn out. But in the case of Eckstein, it turned out to be a perfect image of our reports."

It didn't take long for Eckstein to get noticed in camp. He was the one sprinting everywhere he went, doing everything 100 percent, even in the monotonous drills during which many players go through the motions.

"I've loved the guy from day-one," Angels center fielder Darin Erstad said. "If there's a definition of a team player, it's that guy. He knows his role and maximizes his ability in that role."

"He's a little scrapper," Angels hitting coach Mickey Hatcher said. "He's been an inspiration to a lot of people. He's become one of our key guys in the lineup. Nothing bothers him and I think players feed off him."

Scioscia was as impressed as everybody else.

"What you see of him you have to like," Scioscia said. "This guy will run through a wall for you. He does a lot of things that don't show up in the box-score, just the win column."

MAY FLOWERS

Their poor start behind them, the Angels enjoyed a month of May that was the best month in club history. When it was over, they had won 19 of 26 games and climbed back to within three games of first place in the division. Everything came together. They hit .301 as a team, and the pitching staff posted a 3.21 ERA.

Individually, many got hot. Darin Erstad hit .361 in May despite missing a week because of a mild concussion, sustained after a run-in with the Edison Field fence one night, and a face-first encounter with the turf at the Oakland Coliseum a day later.

Tim Salmon, Troy Glaus and Garret Anderson each hit six home runs in the month. Pitchers Kevin Appier, Ramon Ortiz, Aaron Sele and Jarrod Washburn each won three games. But just as Scioscia had preached to his club when it started out so poorly, the philosophy coming from his office would remain the same.

Don't look back, don't look ahead. All that matters is that day's game. No one epitomized that philosophy more than Erstad, who had no other choice but to play the game that way. His career had already gone through extreme highs and lows, so finding that happy medium became of utmost importance to him.

The Angels center fielder is a crowd favorite and admired by his teammates for his work ethic and hustle, but there is one person in the Angels clubhouse who might have a problem with him. That would be the Angels' equipment manager, who no doubt has his hands full getting the dirt and grass stains out of Erstad's uniform every night.

Rarely does a game go by when Erstad isn't diving for a ball or slamming his body into the fence in an effort to catch a ball. He literally risks life and limb in an effort to win. That was evident when he wound up in the hospital with a concussion, the result of couple of all-out attempts at catching fly balls.

It's the kind of attitude that a player either has or he doesn't, and with Erstad, it all began with his upbringing in Jamestown, North Dakota. Even though Erstad spends much of his time in Southern California playing for the Angels, it's the Midwest he calls home.

"It probably started with my grandparents," Erstad said of his work ethic. "Working on the farm, getting dirty and getting after it. My folks inherited that work ethic and passed it down to us kids. You just take pride in what you do. You start a job, you finish it. They never said that to me, it's just the way it was. It's just the norm in North Dakota."

Erstad played baseball, football, hockey and ran track growing up in North Dakota, and moved on to the University of Nebraska, where he played baseball and football. Baseball was his sport, but he had an opportunity to play for Tom Osborne's national championship football team, something he couldn't pass up.

Erstad was the team's punter and place-kicker, though he could have played more regularly as a defensive back. When Osborne asked him if he wanted a bigger role on the team, Erstad declined.

"I would have had to spend a year in the weight room to get bigger, but I didn't want to do that because I knew baseball was my best sport," he said.

It was the right move because Erstad was the top pick by the Angels in the 1995 draft. Erstad has become a two-time All-Star and a team leader, even if it was not something he sought.

"My role is to play center field, hit second (in the batting order) and be myself," he said. "I expect to play every game hard every day. I only want to be myself and whatever comes out, comes out."

"Darin's motivation has not changed since he put on a baseball uniform as a kid," Scioscia said. "He's all about winning."

JUNE

The Angels played their final two games of May and first two of June in Minnesota against the Twins. Each team won two games in the series and gained respect for one other in the process. It was a hard-fought series played by two similar clubs, and little did they know it at the time, gave fans a preview of the American League Championship Series.

"Any time you come away from here with a win, it's going to give you a lift," Scioscia said after a victory in the final game of the series. "We played a very tough club. I hope they're saying the same thing about us. I think both clubs showed neither club is going to quit."

A week later, a 7-4 win over the Cincinnati Reds in an interleague game brought the Angels to within one game of first place in the division. The remained one game out for the next eight days, but could not catch the Mariners.

Though they wouldn't be able to catch them before the end of June, the Angels found something else that would pay off later. Forced to call up a pitcher from the minor leagues because of a doubleheader, the Angels promoted rookie right-hander John Lackey.

Lackey was 8-2 with a 2.57 ERA at Class-AAA Salt Lake and club officials believed he had not only a good arm but the mental toughness to make his major league debut in his home state of Texas against the Rangers, a team he grew up rooting for. He lost the game, 3-2, but pitched well while lasting seven innings. He was sent back to the minors after the game, but returned to the big club a week later to replace Scott Schoeneweis in the starting rotation. Schoeneweis went to the bullpen, and Lackey finished the season 9-4 with a 3.66 ERA in 18 regular-season starts. His biggest start, however, was yet to come.

The Angels finished the month 17-12 and were 47-33 overall, 4 1/2 games behind the Mariners in the division. The Angels had proven they were a team with good players, so it was disappointing to many when they learned that only one was going to the All-Star Game to be played July 9 in Milwaukee.

Left fielder Garret Anderson, hitting .291 with 15 homers and 63 RBIs at the break, was named to the American League All-Star team for the first time in his career. Before he got notice, though, Anderson wasn't counting on it. He had been disappointed before.

"There's politics involved, and that takes the fun out of it," Anderson said. "I thought I had a case (in 2001) but I didn't get picked. There were a lot of guys like that, I wasn't the only one. The coaches take care of their own, and it kind of takes the luster out of it."

Picking the All-Star reserves is a duty performed by the American League manager. That manager is the manager of the defending league champion. And in the case of the American League, it was Yankees manager Joe Torre. Scioscia, who was named to the All-Star coaching staff in 2002 and would be the 2003 A.L. manager, was careful not to criticize Torre.

"The thing about the All-Star team is there are always guys left off that are deserving," Scioscia said. "Joe knows baseball."

Anderson went 0 for 4 in the All-Star Game, but his and every other player's individual performance was lost in the controversial outcome—a tie game. More important to the Angels, the second half of the season was about to begin.

No Angel player could appreciate the 2002 season like Tim Salmon.

6

Stretch Run

The Angels continued to play well into July. They put together a five-game winning streak sandwiched around the All-Star break to improve to a season-best 18 games over .500 at 53-35. But they still trailed the division-leading Mariners by three games.

The Angels remained close, biding their time until getting the chance to face the Mariners head-to-head. They invited the Mariners to Edison Field for a three-game series starting July 19, and immediately let it be known they were no fluke. They routed the Mariners in the first game of the series, 15-3, then went on to sweep the series to move within one game of first place.

After taking two of three from Oakland, the Angels went north to Seattle for a series against the Mariners. And after winning the first game of the series behind pitcher John Lackey, 8-0, the Angels had caught the Mariners and were tied for first place. They split the next two games of the series and left town in a first-place tie.

The Angels lost two of three to the Boston Red Sox to finish July, falling two games behind. But it set the stage for the final two critical months of the regular season.

As August began, it was evident that this had been a season in which the Angels finally seemed to be having things fall their way. In other words, there were no serious injuries. No one fell into the dugout and tweaked his ankle, no one tore ligaments in his thumb sliding into second base. No freak accidents, as had been so prevalent in seasons past with this club.

On Aug. 10, though, that good fortune changed. Right fielder Tim Salmon, bouncing back from the worst season of his career in 2001, was hit on the left hand by a pitch in Toronto. Salmon immediately feared the worst, believing it was broken. Fortunately for him and the club, there was no break. But there was a deep bone bruise, and Salmon would be out until September.

Losing Salmon for an extended period would be the club's first big test, playing without one of its top run-producers at the most critical time of the season. But without Salmon, the Angels didn't lose any ground in the standings, remaining exactly 3 1/2 games out of first. And in fact the Angels won 13 of 19 games without him, improving to 81-54 by the end of August.

A MAN CALLED FISH

Ever since Tim Salmon first broke into the big leagues late in the 1992 season, he's been the ultimate role model/teammate/employee. On the field, he was the Rookie of the Year in 1993 and has averaged nearly 30 homers and 100 RBIs throughout his career. Off the field, he's been involved with numerous charities and fund-raising organizations. He organized chapel for the club every Sunday during the season and was well respected by his teammates, coaches and everyone else in the organization. But Salmon came to a crossroads in his career when his contract with the Angels was set to expire after the 2001 season. He entered spring training in 2001 having played his entire career with the Angels, and it was a place he wanted to stay. On the other hand, Salmon's home was in the Phoenix area, where he grew up. His wife and four children were his top priority, so he seriously thought about becoming a free agent and signing with the Arizona Diamondbacks. That is, if the Angels didn't trade him there first.

It never happened. In March of 2001, Salmon signed a four-year contract extension that would kick in beginning with the 2002 season and pay him $40 million. Salmon, it seemed, would be an Angel his entire career. Allowing Salmon to leave would have been equivalent to the Padres allowing Tony Gwynn to leave, based on his commitment to the team and community.

"Timmy's not only a professional, but he's an extremely talented professional," Scioscia said. "That combination is tremendous. Tim makes every player around him better."

"I always felt if you had a chance to stay in the same place your whole career, it would be something special," Salmon said. "It's like in college where you have an alma mater. It's something you're behind. That's what I have with the Angels. I really feel it's a part of my family. I look around and see coaches I saw when I was in A-ball scuffling. It's nice to have those long-lasting relationships."

By signing with the Angels when he did, Salmon missed an opportunity to see how much he could have commanded as a free agent.

"The way the market's shaping up, it would probably put him at $12-13 million per year," said Ted Updike, Salmon's agent. "His decision to stay has effectively cost him $6-10 million, or more. His goal has never been to get top dollar.

He wants to play the game and be compensated fairly in the industry he's in....We didn't approach it saying, 'These are our demands.' Our approach was, 'Where do we fit in?' I wish there were more Tim Salmon-type stories in the sports pages. To find stories like his you have to go to Readers Digest."

Salmon, though, had doubts during the off-season about where he wanted to be the rest of his career. He was concerned about the direction of the club and its commitment to winning, and put negotiations on hold. But when he was in Orange County for his charity golf tournament in early February of 2001, Salmon stopped by the Angels offices and spoke with general manager Bill Stoneman. Soon after, Salmon gave Updike the go-ahead to begin negotiations.

"I didn't consider it a conversation, I considered it an opportunity to talk and to share some of my own views, and he shared his," Stoneman said. "I'm not the sort of person who's open with what I'm going to do tomorrow, and sometimes that gets in the way of what I want to accomplish....I guess what I said to him was what he wanted to hear."

"The real turning point was meeting with Bill and discussing the issues," Salmon said. "It was nice to see a philosophy and a game plan, and being let in on that vision."

Salmon said he was concerned that the club was going to go through a rebuilding phase and essentially forego winning in the immediate future. But Stoneman convinced him that while the club still wanted to build from within their own system, they were also intent on trying to win immediately by locking up their big-name players.

"When you're going to do a long-term deal, you have to concern yourself with what the team is going to look like three or four years down the road," Salmon said. "We have a young pitching staff that's full of potential, and there's a lot to be excited about from a lineup standpoint."

Scioscia also played a significant role in keeping Salmon in Anaheim, talking to him often during the previous winter.

"I think it's big for the organization," Scioscia said. "It certainly indicates a direction that Bill's going with the club. Nobody wanted him to leave and we can see he wanted to stay."

With all that Salmon had already achieved while with the organization, including becoming the club's all-time home run hitter, his biggest hits were yet to come.

DOWN THE STRETCH

The Angels had been a franchise haunted by September failures. In the previous 41 years of franchise history, the Angels had a winning September only 14 times. In recent history, the Angels had a winning September only once in the previous nine seasons. The 2002 season would be different.

The Angels won their first seven games in September, and combined with three consecutive wins to end August, they had a 10-game winning streak, matching their second longest in club history, one short of the club record of 11 set in 1964. The streak ended with a 2-1 loss to Oakland on Sept. 9, but the Angels were hit with news that could have thwarted their momentum and even their season. After all, this was a franchise that had certain problems off the field come at the worst possible time, like Tony Phillips' drug arrest in 1997.

The Angels were jolted with the news on Sept. 10 that pitcher Jarrod Washburn was being investigated for his alleged involvement in a sexual assault. But after a 10-day investigation, no charges were filed.

"It's been difficult, but I'm happy to have my attention back on the field," Washburn said. "That's where it belongs. It's not easy. You hear about things like this happening to professional athletes, but you never think it can happen to yourself."

"It's surprising the investigation was the length that it was," said Scott Boras, Washburn's agent. "Unfortunately the allegations acknowledging an investigation became public prior to the DA's evaluation. There was no legal basis to support any claims of any violations by Jarrod Washburn.

"Unfortunately, the burden of proof is switched to you when you're a public figure. It's a reversal of the system. A burden of proof is placed on the athlete that leads to speculation and a stigma."

Unaffected by the distraction, the Angels responded by winning their next six in a row. In winning 16 of 17 games, the Angels were 94-55 and in sole possession of first place for the first time all season. The 94 wins were a club record.

With their first playoff berth in 16 years within reach, however, the Angels lost three of four in Oakland. On Sept. 20, they beat Seattle, 8-1, and needed just one more victory to clinch a spot in the postseason. What a bad time for a losing streak to start.

The Angels lost the next two in Seattle, then two more in Texas and were beginning to appear a little tight. In Texas, the visiting clubhouse attendants put protective plastic above the players' cubicles in preparation for a champagne-soaked celebration. Feeling the players had enough hanging over their heads, Scioscia instructed the attendants to forego the plastic.

Despite their four-game losing streak, the Angels were still in position to clinch a playoff spot if the A's could beat the Mariners, which would mathematically eliminate the 2001 A.L. West champs one season after their record 116 wins. It didn't happen, and the Angels arrived at the ballpark Sept. 26 with that same, "One win, we're in" attitude.

Rookie pitcher John Lackey, who happened to be on the mound for so many of the Angels' biggest wins, started that night against the Rangers. Lackey pitched well, but the key play of the game came from the club's quiet MVP. In the fifth inning, the Angels held a 3-2 lead when Garret Anderson belted a three-run home run. That made it 6-2 and seemed to make the rest of the team relax. They went on to a 10-5 win and proceeded to let out years of frustration with a wild celebration in the visiting clubhouse at The Ballpark in Arlington.

Many players credited Scioscia for creating a winning atmosphere, but he deflected the praise back onto the players.

"A lot of guys here have played a long time and been close but haven't gotten there," Scioscia said. "It's a tremendous moment for the guys who have had some tough Septembers when it looked like they'd make the playoffs, but didn't get there. I'm proud of them; they did it."

Some of those players thought about a few of their ex-teammates, like Chuck Finley and Gary DiSarcina, who had been through the rough times but were not able to experience the success.

Veterans Tim Salmon, Troy Percival and Darin Erstad huddled in a corner of the clubhouse with a cell phone. They were calling DiSarcina, who retired earlier that season while trying to make a comeback with the Boston Red Sox. DiSarcina, who played with the Angels from 1989-2001, didn't answer the phone, so the trio left a message.

"He missed out on this and we remember him today," Salmon said. "In '95 we should have been doing this. And there's Finley. You think about guys who were part of the organization."

Percival said he felt the same way.

"There are a lot of ghosts I'm carrying with me," an emotional Percival said. "There are a lot of guys I'm thinking about right now. Chuck Finley, Gary DiSarcina. They're here with me right now.

"A lot of young guys don't know what it took to get here," Percival continued. "Hopefully they'll never have to go that long. But this makes everything I've ever lived for worth it. This is the best feeling I've ever had."

Nobody seemed to enjoy watching the players celebrate as much as bench coach Joe Maddon, who began his career with the Angel organization in 1981 and remembered many of the current players when they were just beginning their professional careers.

"You try not to be overly emotional, but so many things go through your mind," Maddon said. "Watching Garret (Anderson) walk up to the on-deck circle in the seventh inning, I flashed back to (Rookie League) Mesa, when I knew he didn't want to be there because he was better than everybody else. I remember watching Salmon at Grand Canyon College and saw him as a freshman hit two home runs in a game."

The celebration also brought back memories of his father, who died earlier in the year. "Every game I give him a seat behind our dugout," Maddon said before becoming emotional and asking to be excused.

Despite the feelings of accomplishment, many Angels made it a point to say their work was only beginning. "We really haven't accomplished what we set out to do yet," Percival said. "This was the first step."

At just 20 years old, Francisco Rodriguez tied a record with five postseason victories, including two against the Yankees.

7

David vs. Goliath

If the Angels qualifying for the playoffs was a long shot, certainly beating their American League Division Series opponent—the New York Yankees—provided an even bigger challenge. The series was to begin in New York, where the media seemed as confident as the Yankees themselves of a Yankees series victory.

Before Game 1, one New York scribe did an unofficial survey, asking other writers for their predictions on the series. He asked a reporter who covered the Angels. "Angels in four," the Southern California reporter deadpanned. So the New York writer shot back, "Come on! It's your team, why not say Angels in three?"

"They're not my team, but they are a good team. You'll see. Angels in four," the Southern California writer responded. And so it was on.

It was baseball's version of David vs. Goliath. The Angels were set to face baseball's most storied team in the New York Yankees, and in order to advance to the American League Championship Series, not only did they need to overcome the likes of Derek Jeter, Bernie Williams, Jason Giambi, etc., but history itself.

The Yankees had won 26 World Series titles, including four in the previous six seasons. On the other end of the spectrum were the Angels, who had never won a playoff series. They had played a grand total of 16 playoff games, losing 10, in the franchise's 41 seasons.

The Angels players, however, said they weren't concerned about history.

"The pressure's off now," Angels center fielder Darin Erstad said. "Now the fun begins."

The Angels' roster consisted of one player—pitcher Kevin Appier—with any playoff experience. The Yankees had more playoff experience in Roger Clemens' pinky finger. Again, the Angels said they were not worried.

"Experience always helps," Angels closer Troy Percival said. "What can you do? It's still baseball. The bases are still 90 feet apart. The mound is still 60 feet, six inches from home plate. We have a good team and we're not scared to go up against anybody."

And besides, as Angels manager Mike Scioscia said, "You can't give somebody an injection of playoff experience."

It had been the Angels mantra all season—play every game the same way, whether it's a spring training game or a playoff game. That might have been a difficult task in Yankee Stadium, where the crowds are loud and intense, particularly in October.

"I've played in front of big crowds before, and the one thing I've learned is to enjoy it," Erstad said. "I enjoy playing here because Roger Maris is from North Dakota (Erstad's home state). I just don't get nervous. Everyone says it's different in October, so I guess we'll find out."

Jarrod Washburn, who went 18-6 during the regular season, was set to be the Angels' Game 1 pitcher against Clemens.

"I'm going to stand out there, look around at the people, watch the pre-game ceremonies and say, 'Holy (crap),'" Washburn said. "I'm not going to lie. Playing in Yankee Stadium in October against Roger Clemens…that's pretty darn cool."

Many in New York seemed to suggest the Angels were just happy to be there—in New York and in the playoffs.

"That's fine if people want to say that," Angels first baseman Scott Spiezio said. "We're focused. Of course we're happy to be in the playoffs, but if you lose in the playoffs nobody remembers you were there."

At least one Yankee seemed to take the Angels seriously.

"The five-game series scares the hell out of me," Yankees manager Joe Torre said. "In '96, we lost the first game to Texas and were on the brink of losing the second game, and you think how easy it would have been to roll over and go away. This is where you put up or shut up. It's exciting because of the danger."

Despite the odds against them, the Angels felt incredibly confident about their chances.

"This isn't a fluke," Scioscia said. "This is a good team and they've shown it. When a team wins 99 games in a season, you can't put any other tag on it but championship-caliber."

GAME 1 A.L. DIVISION SERIES

The Angels were a mere four outs away from a 5-4 win when Angels manager Mike Scioscia decided against going to closer Troy Percival with two outs in the eighth, instead sticking with the no-name relievers that helped the Angels get that far.

Angels reliever Ben Weber replaced starter Jarrod Washburn to start the eighth and retired the first two batters before walking both Alfonso Soriano and Derek Jeter. But instead of going to Percival with the tying run in scoring position, Scioscia went to lefty Scott Schoeneweis, who gave up a two-out, game-tying single to Jason Giambi. Then Brendan Donnelly surrendered the biggest of the Yankees' four home runs that evening, a three-run blast by Bernie Williams that sent the Angels into the big city muttering to themselves after an 8-5 loss.

"We got beat tonight," said Angels center fielder Darin Erstad, who had three hits, stole a base and scored a run. "They have great players and they came through when they had to. It's just great players making great plays."

Not surprisingly, Scioscia faced the second-guessers after the game, asking why he didn't bring in Percival to face Giambi. Percival had faced Giambi six times in his career, striking him out five times and walking him once. Against Schoeneweis, Giambi was 5 for 20.

"I didn't mind Schoeny against Giambi, he's done a good job the times he's faced Jason," Scioscia explained. "He made a good pitch. Jason's strong. He didn't get all of it, but he got enough of it."

The ball was hit sharply to the right of first baseman Scott Spiezio, who tried to backhand the one-hopper. But it deflected off his glove and into right field, allowing Soriano to score from second and tie the game at 5.

Up next was Williams, and in came Donnelly, a rookie at the age of 31. On a 2-2 count, Williams sent the ball far and deep into the right-field bleachers, and all was right again in the Yankee Kingdom.

Giambi, playing in his first playoff game in a Yankees uniform, said he believed it was supposed to happen that way.

"That's what postseason magic is all about," Giambi said. "You always want to say, well, it can't be magic, it's not this, it's not that, not the mystique. But the ballclub, the pinstripes...they find a way somehow to get the rally going. Incredible.

"I was telling (first-base coach Lee Mazzilli), 'Thank God I'm in this dugout, not in the other one this time.' Because I've been there two times going, 'Oh (expletive). Here we go again. It's unbelievable. It's like clockwork."

That clock was about to strike midnight for the Yankees.

GAME 2 ALDS

There went the Angels' only chance to steal the series. A blown lead late in Game 1 surely would take the spirit right out of those Angels. Only nobody told the Angels. Though the New York papers had a field day ripping Scioscia and writing the Angels epitaph on their 2002 season, the Angels seemed in remarkably good spirits when they arrived at Yankee Stadium for Game 2.

After all, Scioscia had taught them to forget about yesterday, and it got them this far. Scioscia, though, didn't totally forget Game 1, because he got another chance to use Percival in the eighth inning. When it was over, Scioscia got his mulligan, Percival got the ball and the Angels got their first postseason victory in 16 years.

Scioscia summoned Percival in a strikingly similar situation in Game 2. Percival wasn't pretty but the results were all the Angels cared about after coming away with an 8-6 victory over the Yankees to even the best-of-five series at one game apiece.

The game featured plenty of offense by both teams, particularly from the Angels, who pounded out 17 hits, including home runs from Tim Salmon, Scott Spiezio, Garret Anderson and Troy Glaus. Anderson, Spiezio and Shawn Wooten each had three hits for the Angels.

"We're still in this," Scioscia said. "This gives us a little momentum now going back home but we've got a big challenge ahead of us."

The Yankees got homers from Derek Jeter and Alfonso Soriano, Soriano's coming off the seemingly unhittable Francisco Rodriguez to turn a 4-3 Angels lead into a 5-4 Yankees lead in the sixth inning. With the Angels staring at a 0-2 deficit in the series, lightning struck—twice—in the eighth inning.

Anderson and Glaus began the inning with back-to-back homers off Orlando Hernandez to take a 6-5 lead. The Angels added another run in the eighth to go up, 7-5, but it was far from safe as the Yankees put another scare into the Angels in the bottom of the eighth.

After Nick Johnson singled with one out, Raul Mondesi hit a chopper up the middle that pitcher Ben Weber tried to grab with his bare hand. Mondesi was safe with an infield single and Weber had to leave the game with a sprained index finger on his right hand.

Scioscia summoned Brendan Donnelly, who gave up the game-deciding, three-run homer to Bernie Williams one night earlier in Game 1. But against John Vander Wal, Donnelly struck him out looking. With two outs, Scioscia brought in Percival, though Scioscia said it had nothing to do with what happened in Game 1.

"I thought the elements were right to use Percy," he said. "(The previous) night pointed us in a different direction."

Percival, though, didn't get the job done without creating some angst in the Angels dugout. On his first pitch, he hit Soriano in the back to load the bases. Percival said it had nothing to do with being too amped up.

"(Catcher Bengie Molina) called for a fastball away, but I said no," Percival said. "I've seen him reach out over the plate and hit the ball. You let him do that, he's going to hurt you. So I came in on him and it got away from me, about seven, eight inches…or two feet."

Up next was Jeter, who was 5 for 6 with two homers and two walks in the series going into that at-bat. Percival got ahead in the count 1-2, then struck him out looking at a fastball that appeared to be a little off the outside corner. Percival struggled in the ninth inning, giving up a run and three hits, but he got Mondesi to pop out with the tying runs on base to end it.

"You expect every game to be close going into the eighth inning," Percival said of his eighth-inning appearance. "They're all going to be like that and Scioscia didn't want to burn me out (by using him in Game 1)."

The two teams left the ballpark and headed for California.

GAME 3 ALDS

The largest crowd ever to see a baseball game at Edison Field came out to watch Game 3 of the series between the Angels and Yankees, but the were disappointed early. The Angels quickly fell behind, 6-1, and surely their luck had run out.

Instead, the Angels rallied to post a dramatic 9-6 win to take a two-games-to-one lead in the series with a chance to eliminate the Yankees in Game 4.

Darin Erstad ripped a one-out double to right field in the eighth inning off Yankees reliever Mike Stanton to score Adam Kennedy from second base for what turned out to be the winning run. Steve Karsay replaced Stanton and Tim Salmon hit his first pitch for a two-run homer that whipped the crowd into a frenzy.

The Angels offense did what it did in the first two games of the series by putting constant and unrelenting pressure on the opposing pitcher. They had runners on base in every inning but the first and scored in every inning but the first and fifth.

Kennedy led the offense with three hits, including a homer and a sacrifice fly. Erstad, Salmon and Brad Fullmer had two hits apiece.

But the comeback would not have been possible without the work of the bullpen, which included starter-turned-reliever John Lackey. Lackey replaced rattled starter Ramon Ortiz, and teamed up with Scott Schoeneweis, Francisco Rodriguez and Troy Percival to hold the Yankees to one hit over the final six innings.

Lackey threw three scoreless innings and Rodriguez was perfect in his two innings, setting up the ninth for Percival, who retired Alfonso Soriano, Derek Jeter and Jason Giambi to close it out.

"The story tonight was our bullpen, flat out," Scioscia said. "You can talk about the offense and the comeback and the hits all you want, but it doesn't mean anything without John Lackey and Frankie Rodriguez. If those guys don't put up zeroes, it's a different game."

Ortiz, who appeared nervous in a press conference in New York earlier in the week, was rattled from the start of Game 3. He was through after 2 2/3 innings, having allowed all six Yankees runs, giving up three hits and walking four, all four of which scored.

Down 6-1, the Angels started chipping away at the lead, scoring two in the third on Salmon's two-run double off Yankees starter Mike Mussina. Kennedy hit a solo homer in the fourth and had a sacrifice fly in the sixth and the Angels were down just 6-5.

In the seventh, Garret Anderson doubled with one out and was still on second with two outs when Spiezio muscled a pitch from Stanton just over the out-stretched glove of the second baseman Soriano to drive in Anderson and tie the game at 6.

"You just keep playing offense when you get down like that," said Angels shortstop David Eckstein, who didn't have a hit but was hit by a pitch and had a sacrifice bunt. "In the dugout we were saying, 'Let's just score one run an inning.' That was our goal. We approached the game offensively like we have all year."

Despite the big deficit, Scioscia stuck with the club's aggressive approach of hitting-and-running and bunting runners over.

"We weren't going to sit back," Scioscia said. "We've played an aggressive style all year. Our club has to stay aggressive and we did."

The winning rally in the eighth started with Kennedy's leadoff double. After Eckstein bunted him to third, Erstad fell behind in the count 1-2 before hitting one down the right-field line to score Kennedy. Salmon followed with his homer to give Percival some breathing room for the ninth.

"Erstad did the hard part, he got the winning run across the plate," Salmon said. "I don't know how to put this into words. This is what Anaheim fans have been waiting for for a long time. And me. It's just awesome."

As high as the Angels were after Game 3, they tried to remind themselves they had not won anything yet. The Yankees rallied from an 0-2 deficit to Oakland in 2001 to win the series.

"We've had a lot of emotional wins this year and come back the next day just as focused," Eckstein said. "We know we haven't accomplished anything yet. That hunger makes us just as focused."

GAME 4 ALDS

The Yankees play in The City That Never Sleeps. But after a 9-5 loss to the Angels in Game 4 of the American League Division Series, it was lights out. The American League champions in each of the previous four seasons and five of the previous six, the Yankees returned to New York after Game 4 without any such banner, with their so-called mystique in their back pockets.

The Angels, who went 41 seasons without winning a playoff series, exorcised the demons of so many empty Octobers, eliminating the Yankees by winning three in a row after losing Game 1.

"Nobody gave us a chance against the Yankees," Angels right fielder Tim Salmon said. "They are a great club. Maybe we caught them on a bad week or something, I don't know. But we went toe-to-toe with them and we answered the bell every time we had to."

If it were a championship fight, the Yankees might have lost by TKO in the fifth inning, when the Angels sent 13 batters to the plate. Ten had hits and eight scored. It turned a 2-1 Angels deficit into a 9-2 lead.

The Angels scored 31 runs on 56 hits in the four games, beating up on Yankees starters Roger Clemens, Andy Pettitte, Mike Mussina, and in Game 4, David Wells. Wells took a one-run lead into the fateful fifth when he yielded a solo homer to Shawn Wooten leading off the inning.

One out later, the Angels strung together five consecutive singles. After the second out, they put together another four consecutive hits. Wooten and Benji Gil each had two hits in the inning. The 10 hits in the inning tied a major-league postseason record.

"Nobody could stop them," Yankees second baseman Alfonso Soriano said. "Every pitcher that came to the mound, they hit. Nobody could stop that offense."

Angels starter Jarrod Washburn held the Yankees to two runs in five innings, but he struggled to get there, making 94 pitches. To start the sixth, he turned the ball over to the bullpen, which fought off a Yankee lineup that was fighting for its final breath.

Brendan Donnelly, Scott Schoeneweis and Francisco Rodriguez set up the ninth for Troy Percival, who retired Nick Johnson on a popup to shortstop

David Eckstein, setting off a celebration that began on the pitcher's mound and carried over into a champagne-soaked clubhouse.

"We beat an incredible club," Scioscia said. "This was an incredible challenge and we came out ahead. Those last 12 outs were brutal. We got a little more excited as the game went on, but for us to play our game, we have to take the emotion out of it. Too much adrenaline takes you out of your game. For us to play our game we have to step back and execute."

As the series developed, it became more apparent the Angels were more than fodder for the great Yankee machine. Few in New York gave the Angels a chance, but the Yankees were left to look forward to next spring.

"People who hadn't watched us didn't know anything about us," Washburn said. "Now they've seen us play and know we're not a fluke."

Many in the Angels clubhouse admitted that beating the Yankees was sweeter than if it had been any other team.

"I don't know if people are tired of the Yankees," Gil said. "They're a special team, a special organization, they always have been. But unfortunately they're going to have to wait until next year."

Angels center fielder Darin Erstad led the team with eight hits in the series, but said the Angels needed to quickly shift their focus to the A.L. Championship Series. There was still work to be done.

"This series was fantastic; it was a mentally exhausting series because every pitch meant so much," he said. "But now we take the next step and start all over again."

Next up, the Minnesota Twins.

Adam Kennedy's three home runs in Game 5 of the ALCS permanently etched his name in the Angels history book.

8

Twin Killing

From one playoff series to the next, the Angels could not have faced a more different opponent. In beating the New York Yankees, the Angels beat the most storied team in major league history, playing in hallowed Yankee Stadium.

In the American League Championship Series, the Angels set to play the Minnesota Twins, a franchise that was threatened with contraction and a team that played indoors on artificial turf. The Twins, though, would be similar to the Yankees in that they would fall by the wayside to the Angels, who were gaining momentum and felt they could not be beaten.

GAME 1 A.L. CHAMPIONSHIP SERIES

While the Angels hitters demolished New York Yankees pitching in the Division Series, they found Minnesota Twins starter Joe Mays not nearly as accommodating. Mays did what none of the Yankees could, shutting down an Angels offense as the Twins took Game 1 of the American League Championship Series, 2-1.

"It doesn't matter what the names are, it matters where you throw the ball," said Angels first baseman Scott Spiezio, one of five Angels starters to go hitless. "He didn't give us pitches to hit. There was very little in the zone where you could be aggressive. It seems like we took the same approach up there, but you can only do what the pitcher gives you."

Mays gave up only one unearned run and four hits in eight innings, retiring the final 13 batters he faced and handing the ball over to closer Eddie Guardado, who pitched the ninth and earned the save.

"The guy threw a great game," said Angels right fielder Tim Salmon, who went 0 for 3. "He threw the ball where he wanted to throw it, he got ahead (in the count) and he got into a rhythm. We were never in position to get anything going. It was more the type of game you expect to see in the playoffs, where you see the pitchers take it up a notch. And today he did."

All four Angels hits were singles, and none came after the fourth inning. They scored their only run on an error after Adam Kennedy and David Eckstein had singled with two outs in the third inning.

Darin Erstad followed with a routine grounder to shortstop Cristian Guzman, who let the ball go through his legs and into shallow left field, allowing Kennedy to score and moving Eckstein to third. But Salmon flied out for the final out of the inning and the Angels didn't get a baserunner into scoring position the rest of the night.

Asked what Mays had working for him, Twins manager Ron Gardenhire said: "It would take less time if I tell you what wasn't working. He had everything. He had his changeup, he had his great fastball moving in and out. His curveball, he had his slider. He had the strike zone, in and out."

And just like that, an Angels offense that pounded out 56 hits in four games against the Yankees was stopped cold.

"We faced a guy that got on a roll, was making his pitches and was feeling good about his game," Salmon said. "It was just like the other day when we got all those hits...we got on a roll and you couldn't stop it."

Mays pitched in Game 2 of the Division Series against the Oakland A's a week earlier and got hammered for six runs and nine hits in 3 2/3 innings.

"In Oakland I just left the ball up," Mays said. "I wasn't able to get my breaking ball down. Tonight, I attacked the strike zone and I was able to keep the ball down. I was able to throw the breaking ball over whenever I needed to. It just gives them a different look."

Angels starter Kevin Appier allowed only two runs but he lasted just five innings. He got outs when he needed them and stayed out of the big inning, but couldn't pitch as deep into the game as he would have liked.

"I thought I threw the ball pretty well to get out of jams," Appier said. "Unfortunately, they scored enough to beat us."

Despite all the hype, the Angels said they weren't affected by the noise in the Metrodome.

"I've heard it louder," Erstad said. "I was here for a Packers/Vikings game. It was much louder."

GAME 2 ALCS

It took all of seven pitches for the Angels to show that Game 1 was the exception, not the rule. One night after Minnesota Twins starter Joe Mays turned the Angels bats into sawdust, the Angels rebounded with a 6-3 victory to win Game 2 and even the American League Championship Series at one game apiece.

Darin Erstad and Brad Fullmer homered for the Angels and the bullpen held the Twins scoreless over the final 3 2/3 innings, capped by Troy Percival's perfect ninth, and the Angels had their first ALCS victory since winning Game 4 over the Boston Red Sox on Oct. 11, 1986. The Angels set to return to Anaheim knowing they could avoid a return trip to Minnesota with three wins at home.

Erstad gave the Angels the early boost they needed after they managed only four singles against Mays. Down in the count 0-2 to Twins starter Rick Reed with one out in the top of the first inning, Erstad got a fastball down the middle and hit it over the center-field fence to give the Angels a 1-0 lead. Just like that, Mays was forgotten.

"I wanted to be aggressive, because that's how we play," Erstad said. "I wanted to put the ball in play and not strike out."

Simple, but effective.

Brad Fullmer batted in the sixth inning with a runner on third and one out.

"I was thinking I had to get that runner in from third; that's execution," Fullmer said. "I just didn't want to chase a bad pitch. I tried to stay back and use my hands."

Fullmer stayed back, used his hands and hit it over the fence in center field to put the Angels up, 6-0.

Simple, but effective.

"Maybe we should hit them one and two in the lineup against Reed," Angels manager Mike Scioscia said of Erstad and Fullmer. "Those were two big hits for us. Those two guys, they stepped up and gave us a lift tonight because Rick Reed is a tough pitcher. If he gets on a roll, you can see after the second inning how he settled in."

Ah, the second inning. In between the home runs, the Angels scored three runs in the second keyed by some bad and good baserunning on the same play. The Angels had runners on first and third when Reed faked a pickoff move to third and turned to throw to first.

Adam Kennedy, who was on first, broke for second and was picked off. But as Twins first baseman Doug Mientkiewicz chased Kennedy, Scott Spiezio left third base and headed home. Mientkiewicz's throw home was on the first-base side of the plate, and as catcher A.J. Pierzynski tried to apply the tag, Spiezio kicked it out of his glove.

"We did everything right," Twins manager Ron Gardenhire said. "We picked the guy off first and we just didn't get the guy out at home plate."

Staked to the early lead, Angels starter Ramon Ortiz seemed much more relaxed than when he lasted only 2 2/3 innings in his start against the Yankees in the Division Series. Ortiz didn't allow any Twins baserunners to get into scoring position through five innings, getting help from the defense along the way.

In the third inning, Ortiz picked Luis Rivas off first base. In both the fourth and fifth innings, the Angels infield turned double plays.

Ortiz, though, couldn't make it out of the sixth inning. He gave up a leadoff double to Cristian Guzman and an RBI single to Corey Koskie. Ortiz struck out David Ortiz but gave up a double to Torii Hunter and a two-run single to Mientkiewicz and was through for the night.

Brendan Donnelly came in and retired the two batters he faced to finish the sixth before Francisco Rodriguez threw 1 2/3 scoreless innings, striking out three. Percival got the final out in the eighth before throwing a 1-2-3 ninth to end it.

Including Game 2, Percival had thrown 36 1/3 scoreless innings against the Twins in his career. But that's nothing new to the Twins. Rodriguez, though, was someone they had not seen before.

"I hope I never see that guy again," Mientkiewicz said. "That stuff should be in another league. That's some of the best stuff I've ever seen."

Said Gardenhire: "Those guys all have different looks. They have great sliders. That was the first time we've seen the kid (Rodriguez). Wow, the ball was jumping out of his hand. Then you've got Percival to end it up. That's why they're at where they're at."

GAME 3 ALCS

A walk, a sacrifice bunt, a single, a fielder's choice, another walk and a flyout amounted to nothing for the Angels in the seventh inning of Game 3 of the American League Championship Series. So Troy Glaus did it his way.

Leading off the eighth inning, the Angels third baseman hit a towering home run to center field to snap a 1-1 tie and lift the Angels to a 2-1 victory over the Minnesota Twins.

Small ball took a back seat for one game as the Angels used Glaus' homer and another by Garret Anderson to take a two-games-to-one edge in the best-of-seven series. While the homers were big, it would not have been enough without a solid outing by starting pitcher Jarrod Washburn, more outstanding work from the bullpen and some big plays by the defense in the ninth inning.

Washburn gave up one run in seven innings before Francisco Rodriguez shut down the Twins in the top of the eighth. Troy Percival was called upon to slam the door in the ninth, and he did, but it took a diving catch by right fielder Alex Ochoa on Doug Mientkiewicz's line drive leading off the inning, and a sliding catch by Anderson in left field on A.J. Pierzynski's blooper to end it. Ochoa entered the game in the ninth as a defensive replacement for Tim Salmon.

Even in defeat, Twins manager Ron Gardenhire couldn't help but gush about the game.

"I don't know how to describe that," he said. "That was a great baseball game. I mean, you feel really proud to be a part of something like that. We pitched very good. They pitched very good. They made some great plays at the end....Does it get any better than that?"

It was a game that could have hinged on any pitch. Washburn worked his way out of early jams while Twins starter Eric Milton made just one mistake—Anderson's homer leading off the second inning.

The game remained 1-0 until the seventh, when the Twins' Jacque Jones hit a line drive over the head of Anderson in left and off the fence, driving in Dustan Mohr with two outs to tie it at 1.

The Angels had a golden opportunity to regain the lead in the bottom of the seventh but fell short. With Milton out of the game, Twins reliever LaTroy Hawkins walked Bengie Molina leading off the inning.

Chone Figgins pinch-ran for Molina and took second on Benji Gil's sacrifice bunt. David Eckstein followed with a line drive off the glove of second baseman Luis Rivas, moving Figgins to third.

Lefty Johan Santana replaced Hawkins, and with the infield in, Darin Erstad hit a grounder to Rivas, who threw Figgins out on a close play at the plate. Mike Jackson entered to face Salmon, who walked to load the bases.

Gardenhire made another move to the bullpen, summoning lefty J.C. Romero to face Anderson, who flied out to the warning track in right field. Having used up nearly all of his bullpen and certainly his toughest relievers, Gardenhire had no choice but to leave Romero in to face Glaus in the eighth. Romero fell behind in the count 3-1 before throwing a fastball up and out over the plate. Glaus hit it into the first row of bleachers in right-center.

"Honestly, I didn't know it was gone until it hit the seats," said Glaus, who pumped his fist in triumph as he rounded first base. "We've all played in this stadium enough to know when it gets cold, the ball doesn't carry very well. For right-handers to go over there, you've got to hit it pretty good."

Glaus' teammates were used to it by then, but still impressed when he did it.

"We little guys can't do that," Angels first baseman Scott Spiezio said. "He can hit balls a long way that way. He's got that freak strength. You talk about Barry Bonds, A-Rod, he's got that kind of power. He hasn't hit 73 homers, at least, not yet."

As for Anderson, the home run was nice, but the sliding catch was sweeter.

"The catch ended the game for us," said Anderson, who uncharacteristically flashed a big grin after making the play. "We've never been in the postseason before and I was told by a couple good friends (Jim Edmonds and Chili Davis) that in the postseason you should just have fun and go play. The hard part is getting here."

Two wins away from the World Series, the Angels had every reason to smile.

GAME 4 ALCS

After winning a club-record 99 games during the regular season and dispatching of the defending American League champion New York Yankees in the Division Series, the Angels took a 3-games-to-1 lead in the best-of-seven American League Championship Series with an impressive 7-1 victory over the Minnesota Twins in Game 4.

A win in Game 5 would send the Angels to their first World Series in the history of the 42-year-old franchise.

"It's all blurry to me, or dreamlike," Angels right fielder Tim Salmon said. "The last couple weeks have been so exciting, there's been so much energy. And we're experiencing everything for the first time. I've been in the league 10 years and I feel like a rookie."

The Angels beat the Twins in Game 4 with two legitimate rookies in starting pitcher John Lackey and reliever Francisco Rodriguez. Lackey pitched the game of his life, shutting out the Twins on three hits through seven innings. He struck out seven and walked none. Rodriguez, the 20-year-old phenom who began the season in Double-A, did his usual number, pitching a scoreless eighth inning.

The offense took care of the rest, wearing down Twins starter Brad Radke before beating up on the Twins bullpen in a five-run eighth inning to put the game away. It was the Angels' third consecutive win since losing Game 1, pushing them to the brink of baseball's greatest showcase.

"Somehow we've got to take (Game 5) as if it was one of all the other games we're played," Angels shortstop David Eckstein said. "If there's too much emotion, you can't keep your focus. But the reason we're in this situation is because we've been able to deal with situations like this all year. It feels like we've been playing playoff games since the All-Star break."

The Game 5 victory over the Twins came on the 16-year anniversary of the club's infamous Game 5 loss to the Boston Red Sox, which featured the Dave Henderson homer off Donnie Moore, so the Angels needed no reminders that the series was anything but finished.

A loss in Game 5 and the Angels would be forced to return to Minnesota for Game 6, and potentially, Game 7.

"One more win and we're in," said Angels catcher Bengie Molina, who drove in two-runs with a triple in the eighth inning outburst. "Obviously, we don't want to go back to their home. That motivates us."

The Angels' mantra of playing one game at a time would be tested in Game 5 like never before, but they insisted they would approach it the same as ever.

"We've been through too much together to get too excited," Angels center fielder Darin Erstad said. "We know the Twins aren't going to quit. We haven't won anything yet."

The Twins had been in a do-or-die situation already in the 2002 playoffs, trailing the Oakland A's 2 games to 1 before winning the final two games of their Division Series.

"I think they're going to come out madder than hell," Twins manager Ron Gardenhire said of his team. "I can promise you this, the Minnesota Twins will show up. We're going to try to get this thing back to the Metrodome and we'll go from there. We've had our backs to the wall, been in holes all year long, I promise you we'll come out and play baseball."

They played good baseball in Game 4 as well, as the game was scoreless through six innings. Lackey got through the top of the seventh with the shutout intact when the Angels offense got rolling in the bottom of the inning.

Erstad led off with a bloop single to center. On a 3-1 pitch to Salmon, Erstad stole second, then went to third on catcher A.J. Pierzynski's throwing error.

"(Angels manager Mike Scioscia) likes to get guys in motion," Erstad said. "I got the sign that I had the green light. If I got a good jump, I go. I got a good jump, and I went."

Salmon walked and Garret Anderson popped out, but Troy Glaus drove in the first run of the game with a single to left. Scott Spiezio doubled home another run for a 2-0 lead. Against the Twins bullpen in the eighth, the Angels scored five runs, all with two outs. Anderson singled home one, Brad Fullmer doubled home two and Molina tripled home two more.

"Who knows if we'll ever be back here again?" Erstad said. "That's why we're enjoying it. Win or lose, when we look back at this are we going to ask, 'Were we tight? Did we press?' Or are we going to relax and enjoy it?"

GAME 5 ALCS

After 42 years of futility, disappointment and even tragedy, 42 years after Gene Autry went to the owners meetings to buy radio broadcasting rights and ended up buying the team, the Angels were in.

Adam Kennedy hit three home runs, including a three-run blast that sparked a 10-run seventh inning, propelling the Angels to a 13-5 win over the Minnesota Twins in Game 5 of the American League Championship Series that put them in the World Series for the first time.

The Angels became the fifth team ever and the first since 1983 to lose the first game of a best-of-seven series and win the next four. Kennedy, who was named the MVP of the series, and his Angels teammates were going to play the San Francisco Giants in the World Series.

During the postgame celebration, Angels right fielder Tim Salmon got his hands on the American League Championship trophy, running out of the clubhouse with it and onto the field to show many of the fans at Edison Field who stayed in the ballpark.

"Scioscia handed it to me and said, 'You've been waiting a long time for this,'" Salmon said. "And I said, 'The fans have been waiting a long time for this.' It's not the World Series trophy, but this organization has wanted it for so long. I'm lucky my (sore right hamstring) held up."

Salmon also remembered Autry and former Angels coach Jimmie Reese, keeping commemorative sleeve patches of them in his pocket during the game.

The Angels previously had played six games in their history with a chance to advance to the World Series, and lost all six—three to Milwaukee in 1982 and three to Boston in 1986. Seven was the Angels' lucky number.

"Ask anybody and everyone talks about playing in your backyard as a kid, dreaming of playing in the World Series, saying to yourself, 'World Series, bases loaded, down by three…'" Angels center fielder Darin Erstad said. "Now we'll get to live that."

For a while, it looked as though the Angels would have to make another trip to Minnesota for Game 6 and potentially a Game 7.

They fell behind 2-0 after two innings, but got two solo homers by Kennedy and one from Scott Spiezio off Twins starter Joe Mays to forge a 3-2 lead after five innings. Given a lead, Angels starter Kevin Appier (5 1/3 innings, 2 runs, 5 hits) left the game in the capable hands of the bullpen.

The Angels wasted a chance to increase their lead in the sixth, going scoreless in the inning despite putting runners on first and third with nobody out. The

Twins took advantage of the blown opportunity, scoring three runs in the top of the seventh off Brendan Donnelly and Francisco Rodriguez (all three runs were charged to Donnelly).

Down 5-3 going into the bottom of the seventh, the Angels put together an inning that will go down among the most productive in Major League postseason history: Ten runs, 10 hits and a curse lifted.

It took 73 years for a team to match the 10 hits in a postseason inning put up by the Philadelphia Athletics in the 1929 World Series. But the Angels did it twice in the span of eight days, also getting 10 hits in the fifth inning of their series-clinching victory over the New York Yankees on Oct. 5.

"I was screaming all inning and the only thing I could get out was 'Wow!'" said Angels pitcher Jarrod Washburn.

The key to the inning was Kennedy's three-run homer off Johan Santana that gave the Angels a 6-5 lead, but it nearly didn't happen. After Spiezio and Bengie Molina both singled to begin the inning, Scioscia asked Kennedy to bunt the runners over even though Kennedy had homered in his first two at-bats.

Kennedy fouled off the first bunt attempt before Scioscia took the bunt off. On a 0-2 pitch, Kennedy made history, becoming the fifth player to hit three homers in a postseason game. Babe Ruth (twice, 1926, '28), Bob Robertson (1971), Reggie Jackson (1977) and George Brett (1978) are the others.

"My first reaction was that it didn't happen," Erstad said of watching Kennedy's ball sail into the bleachers. "I had to get on deck to get myself ready and I nearly passed out."

The onslaught continued from there and it didn't stop until the Angels had sent 15 batters to the plate. Naturally, Twins manager Ron Gardenhire came away impressed with the Angels.

"When the Oakland A's ran off 20 games in a row and when they got finished with their 20-game streak and these guys (Angels) were, what, two games back, I knew that these guys were for real," Gardenhire said. "That's a great baseball team right there. You compare them to all the other lions and tigers in this game, they've got big hearts, they never stop playing."

Troy Glaus' two-run double in the eighth inning of Game 6 capped a
rally from a 5-0 deficit. Glaus was named Series MVP.

9

World Serious

To understand Mike Scioscia is to know that he is balanced in life, and it translates into how he runs a baseball team. On the day before Game 1 of the World Series, after the Angels finished their workout, Scioscia rushed to get dressed and go home. After all, he had a big day ahead of him.

It would start with his son Matt's flag-football game at 9 a.m. Then it was on to Edison Field for Game 1 of the 2002 World Series between his Angels and the San Francisco Giants.

To everyone else it was not just another day, not just another game. But Scioscia's approach was the same as it had been since pitchers and catchers reported for spring training in February, and that's how he wanted his players to look at it.

"There's no such thing as stepping up your game in the World Series," Scioscia said. "It's executing the same way you did all year long to get to this level. Our guys are in their element when they're playing their style of game, and that's what you want them to bring."

That philosophy worked in Anaheim in the 2002 season. The Angels won 99 games during the regular season to earn the American League wild-card spot. They beat the New York Yankees in the Division Series and the Minnesota Twins in the American League Championship Series to reach the World Series for the first time in club history.

"We've trained our minds since day-one of spring training to approach everything the same regardless of the situation," Angels center fielder Darin Erstad said. "It didn't matter if we were playing a division-leader or a team with a lesser record. You respect everybody equally."

Respecting everybody equally was going to be a stretch when it came to dealing with Giants left fielder Barry Bonds. A year after hitting a record 73 homers, Bonds set a major league record in 2002 with 198 walks while winning the

National League batting title with a .370 average. The respect he gets from opposing pitchers is off the charts.

"Last year and this year he's had the two best seasons in the history of baseball," Scioscia said. "There's nobody that can look at his numbers—on-base percentage, slugging percentage, the home runs, to the impact he's had on games—and say that anyone has had better seasons in the history of the game. I don't know how you can argue that."

Scioscia was also quick to point out that the Giants were more than Bonds. They won 95 games to earn the NL wild-card spot, then beat the Atlanta Braves in the Division Series and the St. Louis Cardinals in the National League Championship Series to reach their first World Series since 1989.

Second baseman Jeff Kent is a former NL MVP. Catcher Benito Santiago won the NLCS MVP in 2002. Center fielder and leadoff hitter Kenny Lofton got the game-winning hit in the Giants' Game 5-clincher over the Cardinals. Shortstop Rich Aurilia hit 37 homers as recently as 2001.

"It's not only Barry but the guys, how they get on in front of Barry and occupy a base or two or three, where they have to pitch to Barry," Giants manager Dusty Baker said. "If there's a base open, they'll probably walk Barry. If the bases are clogged, they have a good chance of pitching to him."

Angels pitcher Jarrod Washburn, the club's Game 1 starter, issued only one intentional walk all season (Seattle's Edgar Martinez). He's the kind of pitcher that challenges hitters, but he said he would know when he needed to be smart.

"I don't give a crap about macho right now," Washburn said. "All I care about is winning the World Series. Guys can call me a wimp because I pitched around Barry Bonds, but as long as we win, who cares?"

The Angels lost Game 1 in each of their first two playoff series, and in Game 1 would face a pitcher they had never faced in Giants starter Jason Schmidt.

"I watched him against St. Louis and noticed he's very similar to (Roger) Clemens," Erstad said. "He has a bulldog mentality, he goes after guys."

Including regular season and playoffs, each team had played 171 games heading into the World Series. Seven more remained to decide the 2002 champion, and the first pitch couldn't come soon enough for the players.

"I think as a team we can't wait for the games to start," Angels shortstop David Eckstein said. "That's the only thing that's normal to us. We're not used to all the interviews and the phone calls asking for tickets. The only thing left now is the game. This is what we've all been waiting for."

WORLD SERIES GAME 1

Game 1 of the 2002 World Series proved there was more to the San Francisco Giants after all. Bonds had been the center of attention all week long as the Angels and Giants prepared for the World Series, and rightly so. But many Angels warned that though the Giants' journey here was powered by Bonds, there were others that steered them to the National League pennant.

Bonds did his usual number with a home run in his first at-bat, but it was Reggie Sanders and J.T. Snow who made the difference in the Giants' 4-3 win in the World Series opener at Edison Field.

"Every day we have a couple guys in the lineup that seem to match up with whoever they put on the mound to face us," Giants manager Dusty Baker said. "It's been a team effort. We've had a number of guys come through up and down our lineup. Like J.T. says, the sign of a good team is when you really don't know who's going to hurt you from day to day."

Sanders hit a solo homer in the second inning shortly after Bonds hit his to put the Giants in front, 2-0. But just as big was Sanders' two-out single in the sixth. Snow followed with a two-run homer to give the Giants a 4-1 lead which was enough on a night the Angels offense failed to come up with the big hit.

"I said all along there are other guys on that team that got 'em here," said Angels starter Jarrod Washburn, who yielded all three Giant homers. "Barry's big but he's not all of it."

The Angels out-hit the Giants, 9-6, but failed to come up with the clutch hit. Troy Glaus hit two home runs off Giants starter Jason Schmidt, but the Angels went 1 for 8 with runners in scoring position.

Twice the Angels had a runner on third base with one out and failed to get him home. Darin Erstad struck out with Adam Kennedy on third in the third inning. In the fifth, the Angels had runners on first and third with one out when Tim Salmon hit a foul popup near the first-base dugout. Snow slipped on the rubberized warning track and landed flat on his back, but he got up in time to make the catch and the Angels didn't score in the inning.

"I don't think I've ever made a play like that, where I fell down and got back up," said Snow, who was traded by the Angels to the Giants after the 1996 season. "It was a good thing I fell on my backside because I was able to keep looking at the ball. I called it the whole way, and kept calling it when I was laying down. Luckily, the net was there. I grabbed onto the net and pulled myself up."

The Angels credited Schmidt for making good pitches in key situations, but that doesn't mean they were happy about it.

"We had two situations with runners on third base and didn't get the job done," Angels hitting coach Mickey Hatcher said. "I know those two guys (Erstad and Salmon) who had the opportunities are not very happy about it right now. They're going to come out (in Game 2) and be pissed off. You better watch out."

Schmidt got the victory after going 5 2/3 innings and giving up all three Angel runs and all nine of their hits. Felix Rodriguez, Tim Worrell and Robb Nen (save) combined to hold the Angels hitless over the final 3 1/3 innings.

Bonds, though, got it all started. In his first career World Series at-bat, he hit a 2-1 pitch from Washburn over the fence in right field, bringing a groan from the crowd and a smile from Washburn.

"What are you going to do?" said Washburn, who gave up four runs and six hits in 5 2/3 innings. "I made a mistake and he hit a home run. I had to chuckle. I said to myself, 'Yeah, he IS good.'"

The loss was the Angels' first at home in the 2002 postseason, as they fell to 5-1 at Edison Field. But a loss in Game 1 was nothing new. They lost the openers in the series against both the Yankees and Twins.

"I'm not going to say we have them right where we want them, but we've been here before," Angels designated hitter Brad Fullmer said. "So we're not going to panic. We're not overly concerned. Certainly you don't want to lose the first game, but we've shown we can bounce back."

Glaus hit his second homer of the night leading off the bottom of the sixth and Fullmer followed with a walk. Two outs later, Fullmer was on second when Kennedy got the Angels' first hit of the night with a runner in scoring position, driving in Fullmer with a single to right to cut the Giants lead to 4-3.

"We saw some positive things tonight, it's just the score wasn't where we want it to be," Scioscia said. "If we play with that aggressiveness offensively, I think our offense will be where we want it to be."

WORLD SERIES GAME 2

Game 2 was the kind of game that might be common at the schoolyard, or under streetlights in a quiet residential neighborhood. The only difference was that the baseballs that were hit didn't break car windows.

The Angels and Giants combined for 28 hits in Game 2, including a 485-foot bomb by the Giants' Barry Bonds. But no hit was bigger than Tim Salmon's two-run homer off Felix Rodriguez in the bottom of the eighth. Salmon's second homer of the game broke a 9-9 tie and lifted the Angels to an 11-10 victory at Edison Field, tying the best-of-seven series at one game apiece.

It was a game where it seemed no lead was safe, and in fact, none was. The Angels led 5-0 after the first inning, but trailed, 9-7, going into the bottom of the fifth. The Angels rallied to tie the game before the start of the eighth inning.

With one out in the eighth, David Eckstein singled. Darin Erstad fouled off numerous pitches before flying out to left for the second out, bringing up Salmon.

"When Ersty was battling, I really felt like there was a chance he was going to get on base, either a walk or something," Salmon said. "I was thinking I was going to have a guy in scoring position and I had to get ready for that. But when he made the out, with a guy on first, it changed my thinking. If anything, maybe it helped me relax. I don't hit home runs when I go up there trying to hit them."

Salmon hit two homers, singled twice and walked once. Though Salmon would be recognized as the hero in Game 2, it would not have been possible without reliever Francisco Rodriguez, who stopped the Giants offense dead in its tracks.

The Giants had nine runs and 11 hits through five innings, but Rodriguez entered to start the sixth and retired all nine batters he faced, giving the Angels offense a chance. Rodriguez needed only 26 pitches to get through the three innings, striking out four along the way and improving to 5-0 in the postseason.

"That was incredible," Scioscia said. "For him to step up, give us three innings and do it under 30 pitches was incredible. That was the game right there."

Well, not quite.

Holding an 11-9 lead going into the ninth, Troy Percival got the final three outs for the save, though he gave up the mammoth home run to Barry Bonds on a 97-mph fastball with two outs. A key for Percival was retiring Rich Aurilia and Jeff Kent for the first two outs of the inning, so Bonds was not in position to tie the game with a homer.

"I threw my first pitch as hard as I could right down the middle," Percival said. "I think I supplied all the power there. That's what I'm going with, anyway. I told myself if I get the first two guys it doesn't matter how far he hits it. Then I'd get the next guy (Benito Santiago). I didn't want to start a rally with a walk."

Said Salmon: "That was the farthest ball I've ever seen hit in this ballpark. Man, he's awesome."

The game could not have started any better for the Angels, as starting pitcher Kevin Appier retired the side in order in the top of the first before the Angels offense knocked around Giants starter Russ Ortiz in the bottom of the first.

The first four Angel batters had hits, including an RBI double by Erstad and an RBI single by Garret Anderson for a 2-0 lead. One out later, Brad Fullmer and

Scott Spiezio each had an RBI single to make it 4-0. And when Fullmer stole home on the back end of a double steal, the Angels had a 5-0 lead.

Any comfort the Angels might have had quickly disappeared in the top of the second when the Giants rallied for four runs. The big blow was Reggie Sanders' three-run homer, which was followed by a solo homer from David Bell.

Ortiz didn't make it out of the second inning for the Giants, giving up a two-run homer to Salmon that increased the Angels lead to 7-4. Ortiz, who went into the game 2-0 in three postseason starts, gave up seven runs and nine hits in 1 2/3 innings.

Appier, though, wasn't much better. In the third, Appier gave up a solo homer to Kent, walked Bonds and was through for the night, having allowed five runs and five hits in two-plus innings.

John Lackey replaced Appier and restored order, holding that 7-5 lead until the fifth when the Giants sent nine batters to the plate. J.T. Snow's bases-loaded single off Ben Weber drove in two to tie the game at 7.

The Giants took their first lead of the game when Bell drove in Santiago with an infield single, and increased the lead to 9-7 on Shawon Dunston's RBI single.

The Angels got even with single runs in the fifth and sixth innings, Spiezio driving in one with a sacrifice fly and Anderson knocking home the other with a single.

"Tonight wasn't a good night to be a pitcher," Scioscia said.

WORLD SERIES GAME 3

Just wait, Giants manager Dusty Baker seemed to say, until the Giants got the Angels in their own ballpark, with National League rules and that cold bay breeze.

The Angels, though, could not have looked more at home in a 10-4 victory in Game 3 of the World Series at Pacific Bell Park, taking a two-games-to-one lead in the best-of-seven series.

Baker promised that baseballs would not fly out of the park like they did in Anaheim in Game 2 when the Angels outscored the Giants, 11-10, and the two teams combined for six home runs. And he was right—the Angels did not hit a home run.

But they had 12 singles, three doubles and a triple, wearing down the Giants pitching staff by putting pressure on them in nearly every inning. The Angels had at least one baserunner in every inning but the first.

Nine different Angels had at least one hit, including three by Darin Erstad. Seven different Angels had at least one RBI, including Scott Spiezio, who had three.

"Everybody wants to be an analyst, but nothing has affected this team all year," Angels hitting coach Mickey Hatcher said. "It didn't bother them playing in New York, and it didn't bother them playing in Minnesota. I can't explain what's going on. We (coaches) just watch and let 'em go."

The Angels batted around in the third and fourth innings, becoming the first team in World Series history to do it in back-to-back innings. They scored four runs in each, giving starting pitcher Ramon Ortiz, often a jittery sort, a chance to settle down.

"They were hitting; they've been hitting the last two games," Baker said. "I don't know…hopefully they hit themselves out, I hope. If you walk somebody, most of them have good speed and that allows Scioscia to do some things. Most of the guys over there are contact hitters. You don't strike them out very much."

With more than enough offense to work with, Ortiz simply needed to throw strikes and get as deep into the game as he could. He gave up home runs to Rich Aurilia and Barry Bonds in the fifth inning, but that was to be expected. Ortiz gave up more homers (40) than any pitcher in the majors in 2002.

"He had trouble with his rhythm," Angels catcher Bengie Molina said. "I think his wrist was hurting him. His fastball went from 95 (mph) to 88. I just tried to get him through five innings and let the bullpen take over."

Ortiz did get through five, handing an 8-4 lead over the bullpen, and the Giants didn't score again. Brendan Donnelly and Scott Schoeneweis each threw two scoreless innings.

The Giants took an early lead when they cashed in on a leadoff walk by Kenny Lofton in the first inning. Molina nearly threw out Lofton twice—once on a pickoff attempt at first and again when Lofton stole second.

With Lofton on second and one out, Jeff Kent singled off Ortiz's glove, putting runners on first and third for Bonds. But the Angels walked Bonds to load the bases for Benito Santiago, setting up a potential double play.

Santiago hit a grounder to second, but it was hit too slowly and the Angels' only play was at first, allowing Lofton to score for a 1-0 Giants lead.

The Angels took the lead in the third, the key hit being Spiezio's two-run triple. On the pitch to Spiezio, Troy Glaus broke from second and was fooled by shortstop Rich Aurilia into thinking there was a play at second. Glaus slid head-first into second, but got up and still was able to score on the play. By the time the inning was finished, the Angels had a 4-1 lead.

The Angels knocked Giants starter Livan Hernandez (3 2/3 innings, 6 runs, 5 hits) out of the game in the fourth. With one out, Erstad singled and Tim Salmon walked before they pulled off a double steal without drawing a throw.

Garret Anderson drove in one run with a groundout, but the Angels added three more runs in the inning with three two-out, RBI singles—one each by Spiezio, Adam Kennedy and Molina.

"The idea is to keep pressing, to keep pouring it on as much as you can," Erstad said. "Regardless of the score, you can't lay back. It's like playing prevent-defense in football. It's not a good thing to do. So, if anything, we probably up our intensity a little bit (with a lead). Killer instinct? I guess you can call it that."

The Giants cut into the Angels' lead with a solo homer by Aurilia and Bonds' two-run blast in the fifth.

"Yeah, Barry is doing his thing," Baker said. "He doesn't surprise us because we've been watching him for a long time. Hopefully we can get some other guys in on the hit parade."

WORLD SERIES GAME 4

Going into Game 4, the Giants had no reason to believe Angels reliever Francisco Rodriguez was a mere mortal. Not after watching him retire 12 consecutive Giants hitters, starting with nine in a row in Game 2. But after Rodriguez sent Jeff Kent, Barry Bonds and Benito Santiago to the dugout in the seventh inning of Game 4, the Giants suddenly discovered Rodriguez was human after all.

David Bell's eighth-inning single off Rodriguez drove home J.T. Snow from second base, snapping a 3-3 tie and lifting the Giants to a 4-3 victory over the Angels in Game 4 at Pacific Bell Park, tying the best-of-seven series at two games apiece. It was Rodriguez's first loss of the postseason after five victories, something that was almost unimaginable only hours earlier.

"Well, you might be a little spoiled by Francisco because he's been incredible," Scioscia said. "He's virtually gotten everybody out. We know that's not the life of a pitcher."

The Angels built an early 3-0 lead, two of the runs coming in on Troy Glaus' homer off Giants starter Kirk Rueter with one out in the third inning. But the Angels managed only four more hits (all singles) the rest of the way against Rueter and the Giants bullpen, and the Giants offense rallied to ensure the Series would return to Anaheim for a Game 6.

The Giants' winning rally in the eighth started with Snow's leadoff single. Snow said having faced Rodriguez in Game 2 helped, even though the results weren't good.

"We know he's good and he's got great stuff," Snow said. "But you better believe you can get him. You can't go up with negative thoughts in your head. Any time you see a guy for the first time, it's tough. Tonight, we made adjustments."

Snow said he looked for a slider because he noticed that Rodriguez threw them more often than he or his teammates expected in Game 2. Snow got a slider and singled to right field.

"He was waiting for a slider and he hit it well," Rodriguez said. "But it was down the middle. If it's down and away, he's not going to hit the ball like that."

The key to the inning came when the next batter, Reggie Sanders, missed a sacrifice bunt attempt. The pitch deflected off catcher Bengie Molina's glove, allowing Snow to go to second as Molina was charged with a passed ball.

"It was just one of those nights when the catcher didn't catch the ball," Molina said, blaming himself. "(Rodriguez) looked the same. We just had a bad play on my part."

With the bunt still on, Sanders bunted one in the air foul near the Angels' dugout, where first baseman Scott Spiezio made a spectacular diving catch, holding Snow at second.

That brought up Bell, who hit a Rodriguez fastball just to the left of the diving shortstop David Eckstein, scoring Snow to give the Giants a lead and new life in the series.

"When you throw a fastball up in the zone, it's going to go straight," Rodriguez said. "If I throw the ball the way I usually do, it's middle-away."

Said Bell: "I was just trying to get a pitch I could handle and hit it hard. He's had a lot of success so far. So to get a win tonight was big. I think to get a run off him is important too."

Angels starter John Lackey found trouble in the early innings but made big pitches to get out of the jams. In the first inning, singles by Kenny Lofton and Rich Aurilia gave the Giants runners on first and third with nobody out.

But Lackey struck out Kent, and after an intentional walk to Bonds that loaded the bases, he got Santiago to hit into an inning-ending double play.

The strategy worked so well, Lackey and the Angels went with it again in the third inning. A single by Lofton and a double by Aurilia gave the Giants runners on second and third with nobody out.

Lackey got Kent again, but this time on a line drive that Lackey caught himself. After another intentional walk to Bonds, Santiago hit into another double play to end the inning.

Meanwhile, the Angels offense seemed to pick up where it left off one day earlier. They got three hits in the second inning, including one by Lackey, loading the bases with none out. But they scored only one run in the inning, Benji Gil coming home on Eckstein's sacrifice fly. In the third, Glaus hit his two-run homer, giving the Angels a 3-0 lead.

"When it got down, 3-0, I just told myself I have to keep it right there, give my guys a chance," said Rueter, whose six innings pitched are the most by any pitcher in the series. "(The Angels) are an explosive team. They've proven that over this series."

The Giants were able to break through against Lackey in the fifth, thanks to Rueter himself, who got a rally started with an infield single. A bunt by Kenny Lofton hugged the third-base line, rolled foul momentarily but was in fair territory by the time Glaus picked it up. That sparked the Giants to a three-run inning and a tie game.

"We knew we could come back and score," Aurilia said. "Actually, I think a lot of us seeing Lackey the other day (2 1/3 innings of relief in Game 2) kind of helped us out a little bit."

WORLD SERIES GAME 5

Since opening day took place way back on March 31, Scioscia had hypnotized anyone who would listen that no single baseball game was any more important than the next. But with their 16-4 loss to the San Francisco Giants in Game 5 of the World Series, that philosophy would have to be scrapped.

The Giants took a three-games-to-two lead in the best-of-seven series at Pacific Bell Park, meaning Game 6 in Anaheim would become the single most important game of the season for the Angels. At least for the time being. A loss and their dream season would come to an anticlimactic end. A win would force a Game 7.

The Angels had to come back all season. They became the first team ever to finish 41 games out of first and reach the World Series the following year. They began the season 6-14, the worst start in franchise history. Of their 99 regular-season victories, they came from behind to win 43 times.

"That would make a good story if we won two, wouldn't it?" Angels center fielder Darin Erstad said prophetically.

While it had been the Angels offense that set all kinds of postseason records, it was the Giants' turn to unleash the lumber in Game 5. Their 16 runs matched the second-most in World Series history. They had 16 hits, including two home runs and a double from Jeff Kent.

Kent's two homers and another by Rich Aurilia increased the Giants' World Series total to 12, the most ever by a National League team and tied with the 1956 New York Yankees for most by any World Series team. The Giants also got a triple and two singles from Kenny Lofton and two doubles and a single from Barry Bonds.

"They had it going tonight," Erstad said. "It was a little taste of our own medicine. But if you lose by one or lose by 12, it's still just one loss."

This one was nearly over before it got started as the Giants scored three runs in each of the first two innings to take a 6-0 lead against Angels starter Jarrod Washburn. He gave up six runs and six hits, his worst start of the season, which includes 32 regular-season starts. He lasted only four innings (a season-low) and walked five (a season-high). After going 18-6 in the regular season, Washburn went 1-2 with a 5.02 ERA in five postseason starts.

"I've felt tired for the last month," Washburn said. "Tired or not, I'm expected to go out and do my job and I didn't. I let all these guys down in this room. I was terrible from the get-go. I feel terrible."

Despite Washburn's poor start, the Angels made a game of it. They cut their deficit to 6-4 with three runs in the fifth and one in the sixth before the Giants beat up on the Angels bullpen with two runs in the sixth, four in the seventh and four in the eighth.

Angels relievers Ben Weber gave up five runs in 1 1/3 innings and Scott Shields gave up five runs (one earned) in 1 2/3 innings.

"The big key was us adding on," Giants manager Dusty Baker said. "We didn't want to hold onto the lead, we wanted to add onto the lead, which we did. We know the Angels are a big comeback team. We also know they're a big-inning team, much like we are."

The Angels were one loss away from the end of a long and grueling season, but also their most successful ever.

"We've been through numerous games where we had tough losses or got blown out," Angels closer Troy Percival said. "But we've come back before. We've got two games we've got to win. There's not a guy in here who's going to panic."

In the first inning, the Giants had Lofton on first with one out when Washburn got ahead in the count to Kent, 0-2. But Washburn eventually walked Kent and Bonds followed with an RBI double.

Benito Santiago hit a sacrifice fly for the second run of the inning when Washburn lost the strike zone. After an intentional walk to Reggie Sanders, Washburn walked J.T. Snow to load the bases. Then he walked David Bell to force in a run and the Giants had a 3-0 lead.

In the second inning, Lofton again led off with a single and one out later he went to third on Kent's double. After an intentional walk to Bonds loaded the bases, Santiago singled home two runs.

Sanders followed with a sacrifice fly for a 6-0 Giants lead.

Meanwhile, the Angels offense managed to make trouble for Giants starter Jason Schmidt but had problems getting key hits, just like they did against him in Game 1.

The Angels had runners on first and second with two outs in the first and didn't score. In the third they had runners on first and third with one out and didn't score.

They finally broke through against Schmidt in the fifth inning and knocked him out of the game in the process. Even though Schmidt had held the Angels scoreless through four innings, he needed 78 pitches to get there.

Pinch hitter Orlando Palmeiro led off the fifth with a double and he went to third when David Eckstein's grounder went off Bell's glove at third for a single. Erstad drove in the Angels' first run of the night with a sacrifice fly.

Tim Salmon, who struck out with a runner on third and one out in the third inning, singled to center, moving Eckstein to third. Salmon went to second and Eckstein scored on a wild pitch, scoring the Angels' second run of the inning. Garret Anderson struck out, but Troy Glaus doubled off the wall in left to score Salmon and cut the Giants' lead to 6-3.

The Angels added a run in the sixth when Bengie Molina singled, went to third on Benji Gil's double and scored on a Eckstein's groundout to make it 6-4. The Angels wasted a chance for another run in the inning Gil inexplicably held up at third on Erstad's dribbler up the first-base line.

Pitcher Chad Zerbe never looked at Gil as he hurriedly fielded the ball and tagged out Erstad for the second out of the inning. Salmon grounded out to end the threat.

Game 6 would be the Angels' 177th game of the season, and most important. At least until Game 7.

"Well, it was tough," Scioscia said. "We battled back. Actually, you look at the final score, it was a whooping, no doubt about that. But the opportunity in the middle of the game for us to get back in it was there. We've felt good about that, obviously. But that's a flat-out whooping. You can't really put it into any more words."

In Game 6, it would be the Angels' turn to leave the Giants speechless.

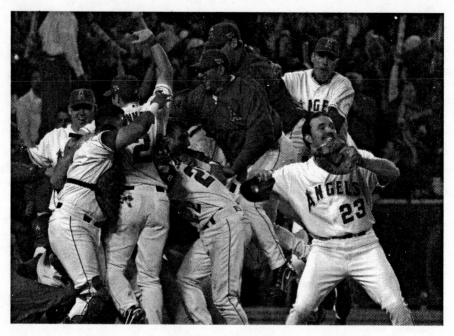

It took 42 seasons, so when the Angels finally won the World Series, it was time to celebrate.

10

Out of the Blue

Down 3 games to 2 and facing elimination, the Angels were down but not out. In fact, with the way their season had gone, and the franchise's entire existence for that matter, winning should not come easy. Easy, no. Dramatic, yes.

WORLD SERIES GAME 6

The Angels could not have been happier to acquire a pitcher like Kevin Appier in the winter trade for Mo Vaughn. The task of facing elimination in Game 6 would have seemed the ideal spot for a pitcher of Appier's stature and experience.

The problem, though, was that Appier seemed to run out of gas weeks earlier. Though he pitched well enough to win in a couple of his playoff starts, he didn't. In fact, Appier had not been the winning pitcher of a game since Sept. 4.

Still, Appier matched Giants starter Russ Ortiz inning-for-inning through four, allowing only one hit entering the fifth inning. Appier got the first out of the inning, but David Bell beat out a grounder to shortstop for an infield single before Shawon Dunston turned on an 87-mph fastball and hit it over the short fence down the left-field line to put the Giants up, 2-0. After Appier yielded a double to the next batter, Kenny Lofton, Scioscia came out with the hook.

A disappointed Appier handed the ball over to Francisco Rodriguez, who allowed Lofton to steal third. But with the infield in, Rodriguez got Rich Aurilia to hit a grounder to shortstop David Eckstein, who looked Lofton back to third and threw to first for the second out.

Rodriguez got ahead in the count, 0-2, to Jeff Kent, but threw a slider in the dirt that catcher Bengie Molina couldn't handle. It was ruled a wild pitch and Lofton scored easily to give the Giants a 3-0 lead.

Rodriguez retired Kent on a grounder to third to end the inning, meaning Bonds was up to start the sixth. After taking a 94-mph fastball for a strike, Bonds unloaded on a hanging slider and hit it deep into the right field seats, putting the Giants up, 4-0. It was Bonds' eighth homer in the postseason, setting a record.

The Giants tacked on another run in the seventh. With one out Lofton singled and then stole second despite a pitchout. Molina's throw was in the dirt and bounced into center field for an error, allowing Lofton to take third. Rodriguez struck out Aurilia for the second out, but Kent singled on a 1-2 pitch to drive in Lofton and give the Giants a 5-0 lead.

Their pulse faint, their offense lifeless, the Angels were three innings away from a long winter's nap. They headed into the bottom of the seventh inning, trailing 5-0, when Garret Anderson led off and grounded out. But consecutive singles by Troy Glaus and Brad Fullmer not only gave the Angels some life, but it knocked Ortiz, who had pitched so well for six innings, out of the game.

Giants reliever Felix Rodriguez, who gave up Tim Salmon's game-winning homer in Game 2, got ahead in the count against Scott Spiezio. But Spiezio fouled off several pitches before working the count full.

Then on a 95-mph fastball, Spiezio golfed one high into the air and time seemed to stand still. After what seemed like an eternity, the ball landed a few rows deep into the right-field seats near the foul pole for a three-run homer, stirring the crowd into a frenzy and cutting the Giants lead to 5-3.

"I didn't know it was gone when I hit it," said Spiezio, who tied a single postseason record with 19 RBIs. "I was praying. I was saying, 'God, please just get over the fence.' It seemed like it took forever."

In the eighth inning, Darin Erstad led off with a home run off Tim Worrell. Salmon singled, Anderson singled and when Barry Bonds bobbled the Anderson's ball in left field for an error, pinch runner Chone Figgins was on third and Anderson on second.

Giants manager Dusty Baker went to closer Robb Nen, but Glaus ripped a slider into the left-center field gap to score both baserunners for a 6-5 Angels lead. Troy Percival pitched a 1-2-3 ninth to end it and force Game 7.

"I've said it a million times before and I'll say it again," Erstad said. "If we're going to go down, we're going to go down fighting."

The Angels had come from behind 51 times in 2002, 43 times in the regular season. Angels hitting coach Mickey Hatcher said he could not take any of the credit.

"They get it going and the sparks start to fly," Hatcher said. "Honest to God I don't know what to say. I'm the proudest hitting coach in the world right now. I just sit back and watch with amazement. They just don't quit. I saw it in New York, I saw it in Minnesota and I'm seeing it now. I'm speechless. I'm in awe."

Though so many seem to feel the same way as Hatcher, the Angels players had come to expect such things from themselves.

"I knew this team, all it needs is a little spark," Spiezio said. "You never know who's going to supply that spark. We knew we could do it. This team's amazing. Yeah, I guess it's the biggest at-bat I've had in my life and the biggest hit. Tonight was pretty amazing."

It was the biggest comeback in a potential elimination game in World Series history, and almost certainly one of the most exciting World Series games ever.

"I can go back to the Kirk Gibson game in '88," Scioscia said. "I think there was about as much electricity in that stadium as there ever was. I think tonight surpassed that."

WORLD SERIES GAME 7

The Angels' run through the playoffs and World Series had seemed so surreal, it made perfect sense that they were to play a Game 7, a term which holds a place in sports lore all its own.

While the first six games of the series featured so much offense, Game 7 was all about pitching, and it was the Angels' pitching that would be the difference. They would use four pitchers in Game 7, including three that were rookies and began the season in the minors.

Predictably, the Angels had to come from behind in Game 7. The Giants struck first, getting singles by Benito Santiago and J.T. Snow and a sacrifice fly by Reggie Sanders for a 1-0 lead in the second inning off Angels rookie pitcher John Lackey. But the Angels responded in their half of the second.

With two outs, Game 6 hero Scott Spiezio walked and scored from first on Bengie Molina's double to the left-center field gap. In the third inning, the Angels would take the lead for good.

David Eckstein and Darin Erstad began the inning with consecutive singles and Tim Salmon was hit by a pitch to load the bases for Garret Anderson. Anderson went into the game with eight hits in the series—all singles. But he ripped a 1-1 pitch from Livan Hernandez into the right-field corner for a three-run double to give the Angels a 4-1 lead.

Meanwhile, Lackey worked his way through five innings almost flawlessly. He gave up a couple of one-out singles in the fourth, but retired Snow and Sanders to get out of it. In the fifth, Lackey got help from Erstad, who made a diving catch on a liner hit to left-center by David Bell.

After five innings, Lackey had made 86 pitches, and considering he was pitching on three days' rest and had already pitched more innings in 2002 than any in his life, he handed the ball over to the bullpen. Francisco Rodriguez, a 20-year-old rookie, and Brendan Donnelly, a 31-year-old rookie, combined for three scoreless innings before turning the ball, the game and the season over to closer Troy Percival, who finished it off, setting off a wild celebration that started on the field, moved into the clubhouse and seemingly has continued to this day.

One fan held a sign that updated the 1979 slogan of "Yes We Can," to "Yes We Did." Even the even-tempered Scioscia seemed to get choked up in the moment.

"I've been in the game for a long time," said Scioscia, who was completing his third season with the Angels. "And I've never been around a group of guys so passionate about the game."

Percival emerged from the pile of bodies near the mound in tears, and soon after right fielder Tim Salmon had his hands on that white Stetson belonging to original owner Gene Autry, who passed away in 1998.

"I know he's up their pulling some strings for us," Salmon said.

It used to be something that could only happen in a Disney movie, and even then it required some sort of divine intervention. But fantasy gave way to reality when the real-life Angels beat the Giants in the seventh game of the World Series, capturing the first championship in the 42 years of the franchise. A World Series title that released them from the Dodger shadow, and so unexpected, it truly came from out of the blue.

(END)

978-0-595-37293-5
0-595-37293-7